MARKETING DESIGNS FOR NONPROFIT ORGANIZATIONS

MARKETING DESIGNS FOR NONPROFIT ORGANIZATIONS

Jack Christian

FUND RAISING INSTITUTE
A Division of The Taft Group
Rockville, Maryland

Published by
Fund Raising Institute
A *Division of The Taft Group*
12300 Twinbrook Parkway, Suite 450
Rockville, Maryland 20852
(301) 816-0210

Printed in the United States of America
97 96 95 94 93 92   6 5 4 3 2 1

Library of Congress Catalog Card Number: T/K
ISBN 0-930807-38-3

Fund Raising Institute publishes books on fund raising, philanthropy, and nonprofit
management. To request sales information, or a copy of our catalog, please write us
at the above address or call 1-800-877-TAFT.

Contents

List of Figures

Preface

Marketing-oriented thinking deserves acceptance, but not dominance, in today's nonprofit environment.

After several years of working in a marketing capacity with a national news magazine, I served as an association publisher and vice president of membership and marketing development. As a private consultant, I work with many nonprofit organizations to increase their advertising, exhibit, and publications sales, and to gain new members while retaining current members.

Increasing revenue through sales and fund raising is essential to the financial health of an association, university, hospital, or cultural institution, but the focus should be kept on the needs of members, students, alumni, patients, and patrons, rather than on the aspirations of an organization's management and staff.

Farsighted executives are not averse to examining new marketing opportunities, but how they use their excess income over expenses sets them apart. Associations, for example, can build a solid financial reserve to offset downturns and emergencies, then funnel the excess back into government relations to protect the interests of their industry or profession, and into producing information and research that will increase the knowledge and profitability of their members.

When profit-oriented thinking is dominant, however, management and staff may stray from focusing on members' needs to meeting personal goals—higher salaries, increased benefits, leased cars, generous travel and expense accounts, or the ultimate monument, their own building.

This is no criticism of large organizations that have the means to fulfill their original purpose and still provide a generous life-style for their staff; it is simply a matter of priorities.

I have presented a practical approach to marketing for nonprofit executives interested in knowing what others are doing to increase their income, and how they do it. Based on my experience and the experiences of others, this book provides guidelines for adding new members and retaining current ones, and examines today's enterprising methods of developing nondues income through sales of advertising, publications and software, exhibits and hospitality suites, financial and travel services, and promotional and gift items, and through fund raising.

This book will be useful to presidents, executive directors and their executive committees, marketing and development directors, membership directors and committees, convention directors and their committees, editors of magazines and newsletters that accept advertising, gift and bookstore managers, and even government relations directors (when additional funding is required).

The book is more than a laundry list of possible marketing activities. If each department operated independently, without planning and coordination, marketing mayhem would result. Again and again, I stress the importance of detailed planning, execution, and marketing coordination.

My thanks and appreciation go to the many executives and marketing professionals from trade associations and educational, cultural, public interest, and health organizations who have made valuable suggestions and contributions to this book.

I. MARKETING OPPORTUNITIES

This is not a textbook. My intent is to provide very practical suggestions with examples for increasing nonprofit income. Local and national associations, universities, hospitals, cultural institutions, and public interest groups are "not-for-profit," yet they also are "not-for-loss."

Nonprofit marketing is not a contradiction in terms. It is necessary to keep organizations viable, without disrupting their original purpose.

Membership organizations will find this first section particularly useful. Since dues account for the bulk of their revenue, nonprofit executives and their membership directors can benefit from step-by-step guidelines for planning, executing, and analyzing membership-retention and new-member programs.

Membership benefits are the core. A simple recitation of benefits will not bring automatic renewals nor spontaneous decisions to become members of an association or nonprofit institution. Individuals and businesses join for information, social opportunities, protection from government interference or restrictive taxation, and many other reasons. True understanding of membership benefits as perceived by various types of members provides the nucleus for retention and new-member solicitations.

Retention programs deserve particular attention, since current members are the customer base. Their needs must be met throughout the year, if they are expected to renew. Publications keep them informed; meetings and special events inform and entertain. Quarterly reports from the CEO add exclusivity. Renewal efforts must go beyond the terse annual notice-with-invoice to thoughtful letters explaining member benefits in their terms—followed, when necessary, by telephone calls. Comparative analysis of the results with those of previous years provides the foundation for future retention program planning.

For new-membership marketing programs we will examine various methods in use today—direct mail, telephone, personal contact advertising, telemarketing, members soliciting members, upgrading members, and combinations of these. Suggestions and examples for every size budget are offered.

Many nonprofits do not have memberships, but even those with dues have found it necessary to explore the myriad nondues income opportunities available today, from the established to the innovative.

While newsletters and magazines are free to members as part of their dues, information is being packaged and repackaged for sale to members and nonmembers. Articles are sorted by subject and sold. Special reports, industry analyses, books, audio and audiovisual materials, and computer software programs are invaluable sources of additional income. To carry this a step further, associations are providing on-line computer services, and training and consulting services on a fee basis.

The sale of advertising is another option available to nonprofit organizations that publish newsletters, magazines, and directories. For those considering accepting advertising, I pose a series of questions to help determine whether it is financially worth the effort. Circulation, frequency, reader profile, potential rate, and potential advertising dollars are weighed against projected expenses.

For nonprofit publications that accept advertising, this book explains how to prepare essential ingredients for a basic media kit, from circulation statements to reader and purchasing research, with brochures that highlight the advertising values. Development of targeted lists of potential advertisers is also covered.

Mundane as this may appear, nonprofit organization executives and editors who supervise advertising sales efforts should understand the fundamentals before they budget for inside sales or contract with an outside publisher's representative.

We examine the various advertising sales methods, including direct mail, telephone and telephone follow-ups, and personal contact. Quarterly and year-end analyses and the need for an annual marketing plan are also described.

Registration sales for meetings and conventions require detailed planning. This book discusses direct mail, publicity, advertising, and even telemarketing efforts used by nonprofits. When associations translate an understanding of what motivates people to attend a meeting into an aura of excitement and interest, then time the promotion, publicity and advertising to peak at the proper moment, they are highly successful in bringing members to their meetings. With the use of high nonmember registration fees, they also use popular conventions to add new members.

To defray meeting expenses, nonprofits are selling sponsorships for luncheons, dinners, receptions, and coffee breaks. The sale of exhibit space and hospitality suites is a major source of nondues revenue for many larger associations, but it can be profitable for smaller organizations as well. This book relates how exhibits can be introduced without offending members, and presents an organized approach to their promotion and sale through targeted lists, direct mail, and telephone follow-ups. Proper selection of an exhibits professional or exhibit management firm is also described.

Through gift shops, bookstores, and promotional catalogs, nonprofits are selling items of interest to their members or visitors. Examples presented here should spark new ideas.

Increasingly, nonprofits are offering special services to their members, many at a substantial discount. Insurance, bank credit cards, telephone cards, and travel discount plans must be negotiated with individual commercial firms. These firms want access to valuable lists and identification with established nonprofit organizations. Nonprofit managers, in turn, must negotiate for quality services that truly benefit their members, preferably at a substantial discount, while providing additional income for their organizations as well.

Fund raising is a subject in itself, thoroughly covered by books and newsletters that specialize in the art. An extremely important marketing element, fund raising is considered here as a major nondues income activity. Most nonprofits were formed through fund raising, most expand with capital projects through fund raising, and even trade associations must turn to fund raising for lobbying support to thwart impending legislative or regulatory threats.

An attempt is made here to look at fund raising from the donor's viewpoint. What are the needs of individual donors as compared with corporate donors? How are special events conducted to appeal to all strata of society? We examine the social aspirations of support groups, as well as the bonding of parents and children through family-related fund-raising programs. Fund raising by associations to support lobbying efforts is considered in terms of who should make contact and how, and the importance of keeping donors informed.

The marketing activities of large and small associations and community health, educational, and cultural institutions are cited throughout. Executives and marketers in associations, universities, hospitals, museums, planetariums, and zoos will appreciate reading of the marketing problems and triumphs of their counterparts. But most of these income-producing activities can be undertaken by other nonprofit organizations with minor adjustments and a little imagination. Examples of various publications, reports, and direct mail and promotion pieces are displayed throughout the book.

The final section is for executives and marketing managers. It considers the role of the nonprofit CEO in determining the marketing structure within the organization, and compares the responsibilities of a marketing coordinator with those of a marketing executive who manages all marketing activities.

Marketing, which goes far beyond "sales" to include market research, planning, budgeting, promotion, and advertising, can no longer be ignored by nonprofit executives and their boards of directors. To be effective, income-producing activities must have strong backing from the top of the organizational chart.

In turn, marketing managers and their staffs must remember that they work for nonprofit organizations formed to serve a need other than making money.

II. MEMBERSHIP MARKETING

Most nonprofit organizations depend on their members for dues revenue and political clout. Member dues provide the primary source of income for the great majority of trade associations and societies, with the exception of the few with magazines or expositions that outproduce dues revenue.

While museums, zoos, symphony orchestras, and other community-related nonprofits may derive some revenue from the local tax base, they too, depend heavily on membership dues as well as fund raising. As the number of members increases, income rises, along with influence. A local nonprofit organization has growing clout with the city council as it broadens its member base within the community. A statewide organization increases its influence with municipal and county governments as its membership climbs, and when members are numerous throughout the state, it receives a fair hearing with the governor's office and the state legislature.

National trade associations carry this one step further. Those representing industries that are heavily regulated or subject to the whims of government agencies or Congress must pay special attention to their membership. Any decline, even in a recession, will be detected as a loss in influence. Testimony at hearings will be less frequent, and lobbying efforts less successful. They must constantly seek new members to offset losses, and concentrate special membership drives in areas whose representatives and senators influence the association's business, industry, or profession.

Membership marketing efforts can be targeted to retain present members, to broaden the base of total membership, and to attract new members strategically located to advance the goals of the organization.

Each nonprofit organization offers special benefits to its members. Before the marketing process begins, examine the benefits for their appeal—tangible and intangible.

1. Understanding Membership Benefits

People and companies join organizations because of a common interest, cause, or concern. They may share an interest in a sport, hobby, or university; they may have a common concern about the environment, taxes, retirement, or bettering the community. Companies and professions may need information that will benefit their business or need concerted action to protect their interests.

Informational Benefits

The newsletter is the communications tool most frequently used by nonprofits. This four- to eight-page device is accepted by members as the most practical means of staying informed. A newsletter is economical, timely, and a quick read—a consistent link with an organization and other members with common interests and concerns.

As associations or societies grow, they add other publications to their list of benefits, such as industrywide studies and special reports. Associations may charge for these reports, but members are favored with special discounts or the reports may be unavailable to nonmembers.

Larger organizations often publish a tabloid, magazine, or professional journal in addition to a newsletter and special reports. These publications, usually monthly or bimonthly, enable members to read serious articles and analyses concerning their shared interests. Though not as timely or easily read as a newsletter, the magazine provides reporting with more depth, and can be entertaining as well as informative.

The ultimate in nonprofit publishing includes books with special appeal to members, audio- and videotapes for training or career advancement, and computer software tailored for an industry.

Large and small associations may offer a personalized information service or "hot line" to members who call in with questions or problems. Some are staffed with legal and technical experts, while some have merely an administrative assistant or librarian who can direct members to the proper sources.

Social Benefits

The national convention and national and regional seminars offer social benefits as well as information. People enjoy meeting others who share their interests. Personal contacts may lead to increased company recognition or new career opportunities.

Conventions with exhibits or major expositions have even more to offer, with state-of-the-art equipment and the latest in materials and services on display. This benefits the regular members who enjoy roaming through exhibit areas, but also brings together associate members or suppliers with their best customers and a concentrated group of potential buyers.

The hospitality suite is an added refinement to the exhibit hall. Exhibitors may invite selected customers to their suites for entertainment, or potential buyers for personalized sales presentations. Suites are usually open in the evenings when convention meetings are not in session. The social benefits to members and the business rewards to associate members may be obvious to outsiders, but they are subtle inducements for members to belong to the association as insiders.

The alumni association of the University of California, Los Angeles, offers members and their families a variety of social opportunities with no connection to business (See Figure 1). From March to August 1991 UCLA alumni could avail themselves of these tours of Indonesia, various regions of the United States, the Canadian Rockies, or Mexico, or a stay at a mountain guest resort in California. UCLA alumni who are not members of the association must join before enjoying any of these social and recreational benefits.

While transportation and lodging are not offered at a discount, members reap a social reward by traveling with others who have shared the experience of attending UCLA.

Government Relations

Government relations and lobbying activities are frequently the member benefit of foremost consideration for large corporations. They are besieged to join innumerable trade associations and charitable organizations. If unchecked, total annual dues expenditures can easily top six figures.

Associations with proven records of protecting their industry's interests in regulatory and legislative matters receive the greatest attention and support. Multinational corporations such as IBM have their own government relations experts in Washington and key state legislatures, but they are considered even more effective when working in concert with strong trade associations.

Each year cities, counties, states, federal agencies, and Congress propose legislation and regulations that could cripple an industry or profession. Individuals and companies need an association that is alert to those threats, with the ability to mobilize its members and other concerned organizations for immediate damage control.

As an example, when a state government recently imposed a special tax on advertising, associations of newspapers, magazines, broadcasting, cable, and outdoor advertising—normally intense competitors—joined forces to have the tax repealed. The state's local advertisers, newspapers, and radio and television stations had objected, but the impact was far more effective with the combined financial and political backing of their state and national associations.

Other Benefits

Association-sponsored insurance plans are another popular member benefit. They range from individual life, health, and annuity plans to company liability and property insurance, all available at special group rates. Members expect their associations to select reliable insurers and to stand behind them when there are problems with claims.

Any number of additional benefits are available to members, depending on the size and scope of the organizations: discounts on long distance calls, credit card interest rates, car rentals, hotel and airline convention travel, and even promotional and gift items. While few potential members join because of these discount incentives, when added together with more substantive benefits the total package can be impressive.

Ranking Benefits

An organization's benefits should be ranked by their appeal to various types of members.

Take, for example, an association with a full menu of benefits and three types of members: small, individually owned companies with five or fewer outlets; group owners with six or more outlets; and associate members who sell products, equipment, and services to the member companies.

The association membership director inserted a one-page questionnaire with the newsletter, which was mailed exclusively to members and outlet managers. They were asked to check whether they were individual, group, or associate members, and whether they were owners or managers. The questionnaire listed all the member benefits and asked the respondents to rank the top ten by their importance, and to make any comments they cared to.

The association's 16 member benefits were:

audio- and videotapes
books
computer programs
conventions
credit cards
exhibits
government relations
hospitality suites

information hot line
magazine
newsletter
promotional items
property & liability insurance
seminars
special reports
travel discounts

Figure 2-1 ranks the top ten membership benefits by types of members. Group owners voted government relations the most important reason for belonging to the association, followed by newsletter, special reports, magazine, and the conventions. They ranked the next five benefits as exhibits, seminars, computer programs, insurance, and audio- and videotapes. Except for government relations and insurance, the benefits they ranked highest provide information.

Although the group owners wrote in few comments, most were concerned with "keeping up with Washington" or "being [kept] informed of industry developments."

The top five preferences of individual owners were not that different from the group owners. Only the newsletter was ranked ahead of government relations, and that was followed by the magazine, exhibits, and conventions. The next five preferred benefits, however, differed significantly. Group insurance was ranked sixth and the hot line seventh—benefits considered more important to individual owners than to the group owners who have their own insurance as well as attorneys and staff to answer questions. Individual owners did not even rank computer programs in the top ten.

Comments made by individual owners brought out intangible benefits not mentioned by the group owners. While they, too, were concerned with "knowing what the government is doing" and "keeping up with the latest" in their field, individual owners also stressed personal benefits such as "being part of a national organization" and "combining the convention with our vacation."

Outlet managers had their own agenda. They appeared to enjoy travel, perhaps because it was not at their own expense. After the newsletter, their primary source of information, they ranked the conventions, seminars, and exhibits. The magazine was fifth. The

Figure 2-1. Member Benefits Ranked by Types of Members

Group Owners	Individual Owners	Managers	Assoc. Members
1. govt. relations	1. newsletter	1. newsletter	1. conventions
2. newsletter	2. govt. relations	2. conventions	2. exhibits
3. special reports	3. magazine	3. seminars	3. hosp. suites
4. magazine	4. exhibits	4. exhibits	4. newsletter
5. conventions	5. conventions	5. magazine	5. magazine
6. exhibits	6. insurance	6. govt. relations	6. special reports
7. seminars	7. info. hot line	7. info. hot line	7. seminars
8. computer programs	8. special reports	8. hosp. suites	8. prom. items
9. insurance	9. seminars	9. audio- and videotapes	9. govt. relations
10. audio- and videotapes	10. audio- and videotapes	10. special reports	10. credit cards

next five were government relations, hot line, hospitality suites, audio- and videotapes, and special reports.

Of the three groups only the managers mentioned hospitality suites, and none of the three ranked books, credit cards, travel discounts, or promotional items among the top ten preferred benefits. They may be additional incentives to join, but they do not appear to be reasons in themselves for membership.

Manager comments tended to contain more personal reasons for belonging to the association, including "meeting with owners and other managers," "advancing my career," and "looking for new opportunities." Although government relations was ranked sixth by managers, little concern about it was expressed in their comments.

Associate members—suppliers and exhibitors—had a contrasting perspective concerning their membership. As would be expected, they appreciated the access to valuable customers, potential customers, and industry information.

Associate members ranked conventions, exhibits, hospitality suites, newsletter, and magazine as the top five benefits. The next five ranked were special reports, seminars, promotional items, government relations, and credit cards. Not included were insurance, computer programs, audio- and videotapes, and the hot line.

Their comments concerned selling and marketing information. Typical remarks were "socializing with our best customers," "being able to exhibit our latest equipment," "keeping up with our competition," and "having access to the latest marketing information."

With an understanding of the relative importance of the association's benefits to each type of member, the membership director was in a much better position to develop sound member-retention and new-member marketing programs.

2. Membership Retention

Retaining current members should be the nonprofit organization's highest marketing priority. If too many members fail to renew each year, the process of gaining new members is like running in place. When it loses old members without gaining new ones, the organization's revenue declines as well as its prestige.

If the only marketing tool for retention is the annual renewal letter with an invoice and request for payment of dues, anticipate the "subscription syndrome." A monthly magazine subscriber may have read eight or nine issues in the past year with enjoyment, but the annual subscription renewal letter is a sobering reminder of the publication's cost. "Can I afford it right now?" "Am I getting my money's worth?" "I think I'll put this off until later." "They're not going to cut me off for a few months."

An association has several advantages over a magazine publisher. In addition to the annual renewal letter, most nonprofits have opportunities throughout the year to meet personally with their members, describe their activities and benefits in newsletters and magazines, send quarterly reports to members, and follow through renewal delays or cancellations with telephone calls and personalized letters.

Association members need to be reminded repeatedly of the many benefits of membership, stressing why they joined, what is being done for them now, and what they can expect in the months ahead.

Personal Contact

Most nonprofit organizations list their officers and board of directors on their letterheads. This makes sense; members want to know who is responsible for making the association work.

Although they may join for a common interest or concern, members are more comfortable when relationships are cemented and sustained through personal contact. They enjoy meeting the leadership and staff, and are flattered when personal attention is sincere.

An annual convention provides the primary vehicle for personal contact. The opening ceremony enables the president or executive director to introduce key staff members and describe their functions. Luncheons or dinner banquets are frequently used to introduce board members. Association members may not meet each of them personally, but at least they can identify the leadership.

Association conventions require tremendous effort from the staff. There are always last-minute problems with speakers, the hotel or convention center, and logistics. With planning, however, staff members can be assigned to attend each meeting, and board members and officers can drop in on meetings on a rotating basis.

At convention meetings and receptions the staff should mingle freely with members. Although it is tempting to confine conversations to their peers and members whom they know, this is a great opportunity to meet members, particularly new ones.

Associate members also require personal contact and recognition. It is customary to hold a private reception for exhibitors prior to the convention opening, since they must be there the day before to set up their booths. Board members, officers, and staff should also attend. The reception is a pleasant means of demonstrating the association's appreciation for associate members and their support.

Floor attendance is critical to exhibitors. They go to great expense to rent exhibit booths, furnish them, ship in equipment or materials, and staff them. Again, association staff, officers, and board members should visit exhibits and hospitality suites on a rotating basis. Board members are normally major buyers, so their attendance is especially appreciated by associate members. Regular members also enjoy mixing with board leaders as they make the rounds of exhibits and suites.

In addition to the annual convention, association staff people often attend regional seminars or committee meetings around the country. These trips provide numerous opportunities to meet with members.

The association's marketing people should be most conscious of members when they travel. If the association has a travel budget for soliciting new members, it is appropriate for the salesperson to visit with regular members between appointments. When apprised of the trip's purpose, members can be extremely helpful by making follow-up calls on potential new members. This makes them feel more a part of the association and may contribute to a positive decision when the renewal letter arrives.

Advertising and exhibits salespeople should also be aware of regular members when they travel. The regulars can frequently assist with information, if not personal follow-ups, and they appreciate being contacted by staff people from the association headquarters.

Some associations maintain regional representatives who attend state functions, meet regularly with current members, solicit new members on a salary plus commission basis. This enables the organization to maintain a regional presence, and provides a source of two-way communication at the local level.

Not every nonprofit organization is in a position to do this. Those with limited budgets hold infrequent meetings, if any, at the association headquarters; members must travel to them instead of the reverse. At the other extreme are the huge societies with hundreds of thousands of individual members, where direct mail is the only feasible means of communications. These Goliaths may be in danger of falling into the "subscription syndrome," where their only contact is through the annual renewal letter. They require innovative communications devices to resell the society's membership benefits throughout the year, if only with periodic stuffers accompanying the newsletter.

Publications

Newsletters, because of their value to members, are an essential resource for member retention. Editors do their own research to determine the subjects of greatest interest to their readers. When combined with the membership director's research on the ranking of benefits most important to members, news stories can be featured accordingly, while also incorporating association activities.

As an example, the association study portrayed in figure 2-1 found the newsletter to be near the top of everyone's list in popularity, and was obviously the most effective means of communicating with them. It also found that both groups of owners considered government relations and lobbying activities the subject of greatest importance, followed by knowledge of industry-related developments.

Conventions and seminars could be treated as news before and after the events. Special reports and computer programs make excellent news stories when released; after they have been available for one or two months, they can be advertised in the newsletter at a special rate to members.

One danger: a nonprofit organization must not appear to its members that it has "a license to sell." Conventions, seminars, and special reports are genuinely appropriate in a newsletter when covered as news events. The newsletter is mailed to members as part of their dues, but other association activities usually cost money on top of dues, so aggressive selling should be confined to house advertising. Ads should make clear that members are favored with special discounts.

Magazines are another practical means of communicating member benefits on a periodic basis. When the magazine is received by members only as part of their dues, association activities can be featured in the same manner as the newsletter—as news events. Association magazines with many nonmember readers, however, usually confine association news to a special section of each issue.

Newsletters, magazines, and tabloids are fully capable of informing members of association activities and benefits on a regular basis. When annual membership dues are low, these publications plus the renewal letter should be sufficient to guarantee a reasonably high retention rate.

Trade associations with expensive corporate memberships have devised more personal means of communicating with members to soften the annual renewal letter jolt.

Quarterly Report

A confidential letter from the president is a reliable attention-getter. It will be read if it is properly executed.

If treated as a quarterly report, the letter provides a trade association with four occasions each year to review the industry's problems and the association's actions and activities. In effect, a quarterly report adds four renewal letters without an invoice. It is considered by many organizations as the high road to member retention.

To justify its "confidential" heading, the letter is addressed exclusively to those who authorized the membership and, in some cases, their CEOs. Although the newsletter and magazine may be sent to top and middle management, the letter from the president is usually restricted to top management only.

The letter or report leads off with background information not made available in the association's other publications. Observations on government regulatory activities, congressional mood toward the industry, recent economic forecasts that might affect member companies—these are personalized accounts that will add to management's knowledge and planning.

The letter can be as long as three or four pages. After devoting the first page to background information on government and the industry, the association president can relate all of the organization's activities during the past quarter. Although referred to as a quarterly report, it does not report on the association's internal financial matters; that is reserved for the board of directors.

Quarterly activities include burning issues; actions taken with government agencies, state legislatures, and Congress—including hearings, testimony, and interrelationships with other associations; brief descriptions of recent seminars, roundtables, or committee meetings; special reports released; major articles or interviews published in the association magazine or newsletter; reports on new members; and any other important events during the past quarter. The January letter highlights activities of the past year in addition to a detailed report on the fourth quarter.

The letter concludes by returning to the subject discussed on the first page, with a commitment by the association president to continue serving the interests of the industry and its members.

Depending on the size and structure of the association, confidential letters from the president may be more selective. In the association with group owners, individual owners, managers, and associate members, the quarterly report is restricted to the group owners. Although they represent only 20 percent of the membership, group heads account for more than 50 percent of the association's dues. Because the groups add so much to the financial strength and political impact of the association, it is essential to help retain these prestigious companies by setting them apart with confidential reports. Since the organization has thousands of members, the letter would lose its selectivity if it were mailed to everyone.

Another association, with only a few hundred members and steep annual dues, however, addresses a quarterly letter from the president to each of its corporate members, primarily senior vice presidents and their CEOs. All of these companies are deeply involved in meeting the association's goals financially and politically; the personal letter is a strong device for retaining their support.

To be most effective, the letter should be printed on the organization's finest stationery, individually addressed to each member by name and title, signed by the president, and mailed first class. Fliers or other inserts should not be included; they would detract from the letter itself.

Although the quarterly report is an excellent means of retaining trade association members, it is impractical for large nonprofit organizations or societies of individual members. In most cases, those groups must rely on newsletters and other publications to showcase their activities throughout the year, and depend heavily on the annual membership renewal letter to summarize benefits and appeal for retention.

Renewal Letter

Every nonprofit organization has a purpose—serving the common interests or concerns of its members. The annual membership renewal letter is more than a plea for money; it requests an affirmation of faith in its fundamental purpose.

If the members share a common interest in horses, the renewal letter stresses the association's continuing role in providing the latest information on breeding, protection of horses through better care, and owners' obligations and rights. When members share a common concern about government overregulation and restrictive legislation, the letter focuses on the organization's lobbying activities, recent triumphs, and the challenges ahead.

After reviewing the organization's basic purpose, the renewal letter summarizes membership benefits, according to their relative importance to various types of members. For example, a renewal letter to associate members would highlight the many opportunities to meet with regular members and to be kept informed of latest developments within the industry they sell to or service.

A good renewal letter concludes with a reminder of common interests or concerns, and the need to remain together. By renewing annual membership, the individual or company reaffirms faith in the organization's purpose, and plays an important role in its unified strength and financial stability.

For members who are hesitant to renew, the final sentence or postscript asks them to reply promptly to the enclosed invoice, but to telephone the association if they have any questions or problems with renewal. They may have been improperly invoiced, or there may be a misunderstanding that can be easily explained or corrected if they contact the organization at once.

Some associations simply ask for a signature to renew, with the bill to come later. That, of course, will bring a faster, and probably higher, renewal rate, but will add to the cost by requiring additional mailings and follow-ups. For the association experiencing renewal difficulties, the signature approach is certainly worth testing.

Some associations bill their members monthly. Instead of sending an invoice at the end of the year, they simply ask members to recertify the monthly amount based on the organization's dues structure, such as the company's annual revenue or total assets.

The renewal package contains a one- or two-page letter with invoice or checklist, a reply card for signature or accompanying check; and a self-addressed, postage-paid envelope, mailed first class.

Membership renewal becomes routine with many nonprofits. The same letter is often sent out, year after year, briefly asking for continued support without mentioning or updating the many benefits and reasons for renewal.

Of all the marketing activities for dues and nondues income, none is more important than the annual request for membership renewal.

Renewal Follow-up

Not everyone will renew. Despite an association's membership benefits, personal contacts, quarterly reports from the president, and concise reaffirmation of purpose and summary of benefits in the renewal letter, there will be cancellations and delays.

The membership department must be organized to follow up the renewal letter, for time is of the essence. Telephone calls to those who have cancelled or not responded should be initiated one month after the renewal notice has been mailed.

Telephone follow-ups are calls of concern, not sales calls. They require intense questioning, careful note taking, an understanding of the organization and its benefits, and the ability to relate those benefits to each type of member.

Calling those who have not yet responded requires a delicate approach. "We are concerned that we have not heard from you. Is there a problem or question that I might answer?" The response should be carefully recorded. If positive, ask when they can be expected to renew and note it for another follow-up, should one be necessary. If hesitant or negative, probe for as much information as possible, and attempt to determine whether others are involved in the decision. "Is it a question of money?" "Are others involved in the decision?" "How do they feel?" "What can we do?"

For those who have actually cancelled their memberships, look for the underlying reasons, not initial responses. Do they still have the original common interest or concern that caused them to join? If not, there may be no point to additional follow-up. If they do, pursue.

Vague reasons for cancellation such as "we've had a budget cut," "times are bad," or "your dues are too high" need further probing. Without the association's lobbying efforts and informational assistance, times might be even worse in the year ahead. Unless a corporation is in such dire straits it has decreed "no more association memberships," it is usually a question of priority. Do they belong to similar organizations? Have all those memberships been cancelled? If not, why has this association been chosen as the budget cut target?

The original follow-up call may present questions that can be easily answered, but in most cases it is pure information gathering to be responded to later with a reasoned letter, and then followed with another telephone call.

The calls may reveal patterns of resistance, problems with the association's personnel, publications, or lobbying efforts that should be brought to management's attention. Many problems can be corrected quickly before the situation deteriorates.

In small nonprofit organizations the membership director and one or two assistants can handle the renewal follow-ups without assistance. Many larger associations have a telemarketing operation that not only solicits new members, but also calls members who cancel or fail to renew. It is important for the telemarketing people to probe deeply, too, taking notes or recording on computer members' questions or objections, for follow-up letters by the membership director.

Copies of notes and follow-up letters should be assembled in a callback file. Then each week the membership department can check those in the file who are to be called again, to determine how many have renewed since the previous contact. Members who said they planned to renew by that date, but have not, should be called once again as a reminder. Those whose objections have been addressed by letter should be called about three weeks later to see if they plan to renew.

Within three months after the renewal notice, most will either have sent in their dues or given a firm indication they have no intention of renewing at this time. The latter names are turned over to the *new-membership* operation, to be solicited the following year as very special prospective members who should rejoin because of changing conditions, whatever they might be.

Recession Renewals

In the early 1980s, associations lost thousands of members in the industrial midwestern states then known as the Rust Belt. While they were reeling under a severe recession, the Sun Belt and energy-producing states were enjoying a high degree of prosperity. An assembly line of families moved their belongings from cities such as Detroit and Cleveland to Houston and Denver, where jobs were plentiful.

Oil prices dropped, dampening the great expectations of oil-producing states, but the defense boom and a generally strong economy brought stability to most states, particularly California, New England, and the Mid-Atlantic.

By 1990 the excesses of real estate speculation, junk bond takeovers, and deepening debt with resultant reductions in government spending brought another recession to New England, the Mid-Atlantic, Texas, and southern California. Least affected were the midwestern industrial states, no longer called the Rust Belt, but rather the makers of machine tools and equipment, the conservative underpinning of our economy.

Membership marketers should be acutely aware of these rolling regional recessions. Companies and individuals that cancelled memberships in the early '80s were prime prospects in the late '80s. Cancellations from New England and other recession-ridden areas of the early 1990s should be heavily pursued when their economies reemerge.

Hard times are not always regional. They can affect a national industry such as commercial or residential real estate, or a profession such as engineering. Nonprofit organizations directly related to those slumping industries or professions need to be extremely sensitive to their members' needs. Consistent member retention programs are an absolute necessity. Dues, similar to advertising, are a last-on, first-off expenditure for many companies and individuals. When times are tight, many will cancel, and possibly rejoin at a later date.

Gaining new members may be more interesting, but retaining current members is crucial. They are the nonprofit organization's income foundation, frequently the source of political as well as financial strength. Real growth is seldom possible without a high renewal rate.

Associations sensitive to their members' concerns and proud of their membership benefits can retain most current members, and are then in a strong position to launch aggressive new membership campaigns that will result in a net increase.

3. New Member Marketing

As with every association marketing activity, new-membership marketing requires planning, budgeting, and consistency. Sporadic attempts to gain new members may result in a waste of time and expense.

Regardless of budget size, it is the membership director's responsibility to coordinate various membership efforts throughout the year. A nonprofit organization may have a staff of only one or two people, or it may have at its disposal a direct marketing group, telemarketing operation, regional sales representatives, and members willing to bring in other members, but the campaigns must be coordinated to be successful.

Planning begins with identifying prospective new members.

Targeted Lists

Valid, updated lists of prospective members should be compiled or selected for rental prior to preparing the direct mail package. To identify possible new members, examine those individuals or companies that have already committed themselves to membership.

Start with all research available within the organization. Use the member retention research to understand how the various types of members rank member benefits. What are the members' common interests or concerns?

Talk with the newsletter and magazine editors about their reader research. They will know the news subjects of greatest interest to their readers, and may know what other publications they read.

If the association has a magazine that sells advertising, ask for its readership and purchasing studies. Consumer magazines will have demographic profiles—age, sex, marital status, education, income, hobbies, and consumer purchasing and travel habits. Business publications will have research on their readers' titles, types and sizes of their companies, purchasing influences within their companies, and the extent of their travel for business and pleasure. The publications will also have circulation breakdowns by state, region, and outside the United States.

If an association magazine or newsletter accepts paid subscriptions from nonmembers, that is a qualified list of prospective new members. Other lists, however, will require more digging.

When an organization is composed of individuals from all walks of life with a common interest or concern, the potential is vast, especially when dues are moderate. Those concerned with the environment, for example, may range in age and income but be better educated than average and be concentrated in certain areas of the country. Obviously, those interested in matters of retirement may vary widely by income, education, and, to some extent, location, but age will be their dominant common demographic characteristic.

Professional societies may not have the numerical potential of organizations concerned with the environment or retirement, but their prospective members are easier to identify. A society of chemical engineers, for example, would not search for lists by age, sex, income, or location; it would examine lists by professions, in this case engineers and, if available, chemical engineers.

Direct mail lists are available for rental. Direct mail directories and list brokers are commissioned by list owners to help renters select and test lists.

Most lists are guaranteed to be 95 percent deliverable, for the addresses are constantly updated. The cost per thousand names varies by size, quality, and availability, but is generally reasonable in terms of the total mailing costs.

With or without the assistance of a list broker, organizations with individual members should select a number of lists for testing in the year ahead. When a potential list contains thousands of names, one or two thousand selected on an "nth" name basis will determine its effectiveness. For example, from a list of 10,000 every 5th name selected would produce 2,000 names that would be statistically representative of the entire list.

Negative results will save the heavy costs of mailing to the entire list; a positive response enables the organization to return to the large list with a single mailing, or rent a few thousand per mailing, depending on the direct mail budget.

Targeted lists with fewer than 2,000 names are usually too small to be tested on an nth name basis; all of the names on these lists should be mailed to. Those with poor results are then dropped from future solicitation plans, while the productive small lists can be returned to once or twice each year until they stop producing.

Trade associations with company memberships present a dual problem in preparing targeted lists. The membership director must first identify the companies that are potential members, then find the individuals within each company who initiate and approve the decision to join.

In smaller companies the owners, presidents, or chief executive officers both initiate and approve new association memberships. Lists are usually available with company name, address, and the name and title of the executive in charge.

Major corporations are more structured. The CEO may have the final approval, but the request to join an association is initiated by someone in middle management. For targeted new-membership mailing lists, the key people in middle management must also be identified by title and, if annual dues are high, by name as well.

Take, for example, a hypothetical trade association in the field of computer security. Most of its current members are banks, savings and loans, insurance companies, and multinational corporations. The titles of individuals who receive the association's newsletter range from CEOs in the smaller concerns to senior vice presidents, industrial security directors, and computer security managers in the larger companies.

If the association has a small staff with membership benefits limited to a monthly newsletter and special reports, its dues would be low and the number of potential members rather high. It could select industry lists for testing purposes and simply address new membership mailings by title alone, such as Industrial Security Director or Computer Security Manager, and depend on company mail rooms to route the letters to the proper people.

Now assume the association is in the field of computer security, but with many valuable membership benefits. It has a staff of computer security specialists available to develop stringent security programs for its members, training programs for company personnel, a highly confidential newsletter and special reports mailed to members' home addresses, and a hot line system of telephone alerts to and from members when there are emergencies such as computer break-ins or "viruses."

Since that association's annual dues are more than $10,000, memberships could not be solicited by using direct mail addressed to the Industrial Security Director.

Instead the membership department would tailor its own exclusive lists, starting with the top 50 banks, savings and loans, insurance companies, and multinational corporations. Business libraries have directories with company names, addresses, telephone numbers, and CEOs, ranked by company size. When this information from the 200 targeted companies is transferred to the association's computer, the membership department will fine-tune the list to those who can initiate and approve the decision to join.

Each company is telephoned. If the CEO's name is Claude Robinson, the caller asks the receptionist for Mr. Robinson's executive secretary. From there the conversation follows this pattern:

"Hello, are you Mr. Robinson's secretary?"

If the response is affirmative, reply: "I am Vera Malinowsky from the Confidential Computer Security Association in Washington. Our president, James Sherman, would like to write to Mr. Robinson concerning our organization, and I am calling to verify his name, title, and address."

Since the caller already has the information and is not asking to speak with the CEO personally, the secretary will comply with the verification.

The next stage is more difficult.

"Is there someone else in your company who should be aware of our association? Who is in charge of computer security?"

A cautious secretary will ask for the caller's telephone number and offer to call back with the information requested. No cause for alarm; that in itself identifies the company as security-conscious. Ultimately, more than nine out of ten will provide the names, titles, correct addresses, and telephone extensions of the key middle management personnel. The few who refrain from giving additional names will suggest that the association president write to the CEO, and the secretary will forward the information to the proper person if the CEO is interested.

Before ending the conversation the caller obtains the name of the CEO's secretary, easing the way for telephone follow-ups after the mailings.

When completed, this highly targeted list of 200 companies will contain approximately 500 names of qualified people directly involved in any decision to join the association. The first new member's dues will more than compensate for the cost of developing the list and the subsequent follow-ups.

The mailing lists have been selected or developed, including the in-house lists of 1) former members who have cancelled; 2) nonmembers who subscribe to the association's publications; and 3) nonmembers who have called or written for information. For outside lists, large individual-member organizations have selected lists of names to be tested based on their demographics or interests; professional societies have chosen lists of names with similar professional interests; associations with moderate dues have earmarked lists of companies to be addressed by titles only; and specialized associations that justifiably demand substantial annual dues have tailored their own targeted lists of decision makers within potential member companies.

Based on careful list selection or development, membership directors can prepare realistic budgets for new-membership efforts in the coming year. With budget approval, the solicitation process begins.

Direct Mail

The size and quality of potential member lists dictates the direct mail treatment. Nonprofit organizations with low annual dues and broad appeal send out bulk mailings to any number of rented lists throughout the year. Since personal follow-ups are prohibitive, every conceivable direct mail device is used to prompt a favorable decision before the mailing is discarded.

Associations and professional organizations with higher dues and potential prospects in the thousands, rather than hundreds of thousands, send a more personalized direct mail solicitation first class. These letters may linger on recipients' desks for several weeks before a decision is made. They are followed up with two or three subsequent mailings each year or by telephone some weeks after the initial mailing.

Small associations with potential member companies in the hundreds and dues in the thousands often send a complete package of materials with the first solicitation, allowing managers to forward the materials to others in the company for their analyses and recommendations. These companies are called and the decision-making process is traced, for it may be months before final decisions are made.

Mass Mailings. The American Automobile Association, with 32 million members, is among the largest and most successful nonprofit organizations in the United States. Virtually every residence has one or more car owners, and the AAA benefits are extremely appealing. Since the number of prospects is too overwhelming for follow-up calls, the organization depends on the mailing to force an immediate decision to join by sending in a check or credit card authorization.

A recent AAA membership mailing was sent by bulk postage rate addressed to "Our Neighbors," rather than to an individual name or "Resident." It contained the following direct mail pieces:

- four-page letter
- "Save $14.00" coupon
- "FREE Road Service . . ." brochure
- AAA car window emblems
- "Return Notice Card" with "Temporary Membership" cards
- Self-addressed, postage-paid envelope

Each element is worth examining. The covering letter is on two sheets of note-size paper, with copy on front and back of each. The AAA logo and subheads are blue; the copy is black typewriter type.

The first page opens with an acknowledgment that ". . . this may not be the first invitation you've received to join the AAA, but none has been more generous," followed by the special offers:

Join AAA in the next 10 days, and you'll get—
- a $14.00 savings . . .
- a second membership FREE . . .
- a bonus gift—a AAA special—also FREE . . .
- a one year FULL money-back guarantee!

The first page concludes with AAA's single most important membership benefit:

Whatever happens to your car, you'll know AAA will come to your rescue speedily, professionally, and in most cases, at no charge to you.

The first page alone is reason enough to join. Pages two and three, however, explain in detail all of the membership benefits offered by AAA. The subheads alone summarize the association's total benefits in their order of relative importance:

Emergency Road Service
Approved Auto Repair
FREE! AAA's Famous Maps, Tourbooks® and Triptiks®
Free Personal Travel Planning Service
AAA Travel Agency
AAA/VISA Credit Card
American Express® Travelers Cheques Fee-Free
Car Rental Discount
Free Bail Bond Service
AAA Costs So Little

The fourth and final page of the covering letter asks for the order, explains how to join, and repeats the special offers made on the first page. A "P.S." finally explains the bonus gift:

. . . full-size, 144-page AAA North American Road Atlas. This full-color atlas is yours free when you join and send in payment in the next 10 days. A $6.95 value but it's yours free! This is the final incentive to take immediate action.

A typical mass mailing package does not depend solely on the letter for a favorable decision. Several attractive pieces are included to reinforce the points made in the letter. Frequently these pieces are examined first and are persuasive reasons for reading the letter for more details.

The four-color brochure is designed to grab the attention of every car owner, including those who belong to one of AAA's competitors. The bold headline reads:

FREE Road Service
24 hours a day
365 days a year

Inside the brochure the headlines and photos highlight AAA's most important membership benefit: *"Get help when and where you need it—5 Emergency Services—all FREE."* The photos depict the five emergency situations:

- Free Roadside Service
- Free Emergency Gas Delivery
- Free Change of Flats
- Free Battery Boosts
- Free Tow to Safety

The brochure's back panel offers a *"One Year Money-Back Guarantee"* that permits the new member to cancel any time during the first year and receive a full refund of membership dues, no questions asked.

The AAA package also includes a "Save $14.00" coupon that explains how "you'll save $14.00 off your first-year membership dues." Ordinarily, new members are required to pay $55.00, including a one-time enrollment fee of $14.00, but the offer waives the $14.00 *"if you join within the next 10 days."* The coupon's reverse side offers a second membership in the same household free, along with the bonus gift mentioned above.

Two blue and silver car window stickers with the "AAA Protected" logo are included, with this warning: "These emblems are to be displayed by members only, and *only* members are protected by the AAA Auto Theft Reward." A gimmick? Perhaps, but the emblems gain attention and are reminders of another membership benefit. Who would not like to display an emblem that warns against theft? Just one more reason to join now.

The reply card is the most read element in any direct mail package, since it goes beyond the "free" offers to spell out the actual cost of membership and method of payment. The AAA return notice card is more visible than most reply cards because it also includes two "Temporary Membership" cards.

Carrying an expiration date of approximately 45 days after receipt of the mailing, the cards list temporary benefits during that period, plus the permanent benefits available only when the recipient becomes a member. Although actually good for 45 days, the "10-day offer" gives the mailing a greater sense of urgency.

The reply card asks for $41 for a full membership and associate membership, and $22 for each additional associate membership, to be paid by check or credit card.

For those who join, the postage-paid reply envelope has a final tear-off bonus offer:

Use your VISA, MasterCard or American Express card to pay your membership dues, and get an extra month of AAA FREE!

The $3.42 final offer is explained:

using credit cards helps us cut clerical time and trim postage, letter and envelope costs in sending out renewal statements and reminders.

In exchange for one month's additional membership coverage, AAA can automatically renew the dues each year by charging the member's credit card account without sending a renewal notice, which requires a decision to renew. This is a major benefit to the association, well worth considering by nonprofit organizations with individual members.

Most nonprofits do not have a direct mail budget to compare with

AAA and its 32 million members, or the American Association of Retired Persons (AARP) with a reported 28 million members and growing at the rate of 6,000 per day, but the principles are the same. Describe the benefits in order of their importance to prospective members, and include one or more special offers as an incentive to join immediately.

The Los Angeles County Museum of Art, with nearly 90,000 members, claims the largest number of resident members of all museums in the United States.

Its aggressive membership department has two or three large mailings each year to prospective new members, totaling more than one million pieces of direct mail annually. The promotion is primarily exhibit-oriented.

A recent mailing featured a Georgia O'Keeffe exhibit. The cover letter, addressed to "Dear Friend," is a single page printed on both sides, with black typewriter type and blue highlights.

The letter is beautifully written. It leads off:

> Brilliant desert flowers . . . sun-bleached bones . . . bare sweeping landscapes . . . and cloudless southwestern skies. These are the scenes we all imagine when we hear the name "Georgia O'Keeffe."

After describing the forthcoming O'Keeffe exhibition at the Los Angeles County Museum of Art, in boldface blue type it says:

> THIS WILL BE YOUR LAST OPPORTUNITY TO SEE THIS SPLENDID COLLECTION OF O'KEEFFE WORKS ANY-WHERE!
>
> By joining the Museum now, you will receive TWO FREE tickets and an exclusive early opportunity to reserve tickets for "Georgia O'Keeffe"—prior to public ticket sales.

At the bottom of page one the letter leads into the other membership benefits which are described on the opposite side of the page:

> And that will be only the beginning! For a full year you'll also enjoy . . . . .

please turn . . .

1. . . . 12 months of Free Family Admissions to all Museum galleries and special exhibitions; single Members may bring a guest!

2. . . . Advance Notice of coming exhibitions through the monthly **Members' Calendar**, the full-color Museum magazine;

3. . . . An Invitation to the New Members' Party, a private Members-only "welcoming" event with special tours of current exhibitions;

4. . . . Members-only Preview Days when you'll see 8 major exhibitions this year before they open to the public and receive up to $72 worth of special admission privileges;

5. . . . Your Members' Discount at three Museum Shops including the new shop located in the Pavilion for Japanese Art.

In addition to the cover letter, there was a reproduction of Georgia O'Keeffe's "Red Poppy" and a striking brochure headlined "Join Us!" that provides a thorough description of the museum and membership benefits, with a built-in self-mailing enrollment form. Another four-color brochure tells the story with its title:

It's a matter of priorities . . .
Priority Ticketing,
Priority Notice,
Priority Events,

This brochure repeats the member benefits and lists the "8 Special Touring Exhibitions this year!"

This is an extremely impressive direct mail package. By addressing this same mailing to "Dear Former Member" instead of "Dear Friend," along with minor changes in the cover letter copy, it was also sent to the museum's "lapse recapture" list.

Instead of featuring an exhibit, another museum mailing was price-oriented. It offered a 20 percent discount plus three months of membership free.

This promotional effort included a four-page letter on note-size paper, a small brochure titled "Your Inside Track to Privileges, Priorities, and a Private Party," an enrollment form, and a postage-paid reply envelope.

Inside the flap of the outer envelope is an information card released by the City of Los Angeles Social Service Department. It is interesting reading for a nonprofit marketer:

ACTIVITY   An appeal for donations to June 30, 1990.

PURPOSE   Net proceeds to support the museums and exhibitions, facility expansion and art acquisition.

EXPENSE   Estimated at $2,849,888 for printing, postage, publicity, staff, fees, catalogues and miscellaneous expenses.

PREVIOUS   1988–89 appeal raised $18,394,177

ACTIVITY   from gross receipts of $20,642,819 at an expense of $2,248,642 or 10.9% of gross receipts.

Membership dues account for approximately one-third of the museum's total budget. It receives support from Los Angeles County and from private and corporate donors. Donors may restrict their funds to specific acquisitions or facilities, while membership dues are unrestricted funds to be used as needed.

Moderate Mailings. The Saint Louis Zoological Park is a venerable institution in the Midwest, well known and loved by parents and children within a 200-mile radius. Also one of the nation's oldest zoos, the Saint Louis Zoo opened in 1913. Fifty years later, in 1963, the Zooline Railroad began to operate, carrying passengers around the grounds. It is known for its Children's Zoo, Big Cat Country, Jungle of the Apes, and a new Endangered Research and Veterinary Hospital.

In the summer of 1989, the Saint Louis Zoo dedicated The Living World, the first facility of its kind that combines high technology with live animals to explain interrelationships in the biological world.

The Living World has two spacious exhibit halls, four classrooms, a lecture hall, and a 400-seat auditorium featuring a spectacular wildlife film on a giant screen. Also in the new facility are a glass-enclosed, climate-controlled restaurant and a gift shop.

Until 1989 all membership efforts were conducted by volunteers. Although the Zoo Friends Association (ZFA) still has a volunteer corps of 600 who devote thousands of hours each year to enhancing the institution, the board decided to hire a team of professionals for marketing and development activities.

In a two-year period, ZFA membership skyrocketed from 12,300 to more than 17,000, plus an additional 10,000 "Zoo Parents" who have adopted an animal and contribute toward its care and feeding with contributions as small as $10. Even more impressive, ZFA has an 82 percent renewal rate!

The initial 1989 direct mail campaign, "See the Living World," was an immediate success, resulting in 2,050 new members. To attract more visitors to the new restaurant, they offered new members a free lunch in the Painted Giraffe Cafe. A second offer gave them "a free night in The Living World, an evening of discovery."

In the winter of 1989, the focus was on winter activities. Tied in with a local billboard campaign picturing four plaintive cheetahs— "We're Here All Year, Saint Louis Zoo—See The Living World," a second direct mail offer encouraged families to join and attend the zoo throughout the winter months, where all the buildings are heated and where they can see the newest addition.

An accompanying brochure replicated the billboard advertisement on its cover. After describing the new attraction, The Living World, the inside copy read:

Join the Zoo Friends Association . . .

Now is the time to join the Saint Louis Zoo Friends Association because we're not just here during the summer. We invite you to weather winter with the *wildlife* at the Saint Louis Zoo.

The Living World is an all-weather attraction, and the Jungle of the Apes, the Herpetarium and the Bird, Antelope, Elephant, Aquatic and Primate Houses also are heated buildings, open year round. The big cats, the bears and the birds are all species with a tolerance for cool weather. The animals can do it—so can you.

The brochure repeated the earlier offer, which had been so success-ful—"If you join before January 30, 1990, you will receive a coupon for $5.00 toward lunch at The Painted Giraffe Cafe and a special invitation to a private showing of The Living World." It concluded with a bold "Join Now—and remember WE'RE HERE ALL YEAR."

The winter mailing added another 1,100 new members. ZFA members also receive a handsome tabloid-style, four-color bimonthly publication called *Zudus*. In addition to running interesting and entertaining articles on animals at the zoo, *Zudus* lists donors who have given $250 or more.

In 1990, the membership development staff sent two mailings to prospective members in the spring and fall. Their new theme featured three penguins asking: "DO YOU 'ZOO'? WE DO!"

The mailings were unpretentious, inexpensive, and effective. A covering letter with one page and copy on both sides described the benefits of membership. The P.S. urged recipients to "join by phone using your MasterCard or Visa charge cards and we will send you a special surprise gift." Those who responded by phone received a small animal magnet, which cost the zoo practically nothing. In return, it simplified the process and saved the zoo a considerable amount in accounting expenses.

Other than a postage-paid, self-addressed envelope, the only enclosure was a two-color flier. On one side the heading read "Want to 'Zoo'? Join and Enjoy These . . ." It then described Zoo Attractions, Zoo Happenings (special events, entertainment, education classes) and A Zoo Ado—the zoo's newest casual summer party. At the bottom of the flier was a tear-off membership application form.

On the other side was a detailed map of the zoo, with a list of companies in the St. Louis area willing to match their employees' dues or donations, ranging from $25 for senior citizens to $35 for regular members, and up to $2,500 through the various membership levels.

Prior to 1990, the list of matching companies had never appeared in Zoo Friends promotional materials, on the assumption that new members would know whether their employers were matching companies. Not only did the 1990 mailings produce another 2,066 members, but the average dollars-per-member increased by an impressive 30 percent with matching funds!

Another variable was introduced in the 1990 direct mail. In the spring mailing, half of the recipients were offered the $5.00 free lunch coupon and the other half were offered a New Visitor's Guide valued at $5.95. The free lunch outpulled the guide by a significant number.

Although only 22 percent of those who chose the free lunch coupon actually used it, the development staff continued to look for a substitute.

In the fall mailing, 50 percent were tested with the lunch offer and the other half were offered a free "Family Pack," an attractive pink and green insulated cooler bag. Since the family pack produced nearly the same number of new members as the lunch coupon, it is used exclusively in the current mailings. The Zoo Friends cooler pack is also given to members who upgrade their memberships by renewing at a higher level.

Three mailings were planned for 1991, with a total of 380,000 pieces. The theme was "for the Price of Peanuts You Can Have the Biggest Year Yet." Although St. Louis city and county provide $7 million a year to the zoo budget, dues and special fund raisers accounted for another $3 million. The 1991–92 budget projections for the ZFA are set at $4.4 million.

These moderately priced direct mail campaigns are imaginative, and are fueled by an enthusiastic development director who understands themes that work, yet is willing to test new ideas and approaches for ever-increasing results.

In another use of moderate-size mailings, many trade associations have at their disposal well-defined lists of prospective member companies. Rather than conduct mass mailings to rented lists, they can cover targeted lists with a series of mailings each year, or just one or two mailings followed by personal telephone calls.

The National Association of Broadcasters serves U.S. radio and television stations. Its Radio Division has more than 4,000 member stations, and a potential additional 5,000 or more.

NAB Radio has three types of members—AM, FM, and associate members. Although many AM/FM combination stations share a location, separate mailings are made to AM and FM owners and managers, since many of their basic problems and issues differ. Direct mail serves a dual purpose—it attempts to induce owners and managers to join now, and for those who hesitate it provides a detailed menu of benefits to pave the way for follow-up telephone calls.

NAB dues are payable monthly, based on annual radio station

revenue minus advertising agency commissions. Since prospective members need send in only the first month's dues when they join, the direct mail in itself produces many new members without any follow-up.

A recent mailing to prospective AM radio station owners and managers contains the following elements:

- a four-page letter
- *AM Update* brochure
- NAB Radio membership application
- Postage-paid reply envelope

Unlike the AAA letter with its two pages printed front and back, NAB has a newsletter-style four-pager that opens up with pages two and three fully visible to the reader, providing a complete display of membership benefits.

Page one is a staccato reminder of AM radio's leading problems and issues, emphasized with heavy underlining:

tough times during the 80's, but NAB took the leadership role in improving AM [Radio] . . .

achievements in the Active 80's . . .

Will this become the Complacent 90's?

Not if you . . . support . . . Radio Quality [legislation] . . .

threatening proposals . . . can have a direct effect on your sales and profits . . .

We need each other . . . each new member makes us more effective . . . we protect your interests and provide you with profitable ideas and assistance . . .

Again, the most important reasons for joining the association are featured on the first page of the letter.

Pages two and three provide an open display of membership benefits, tangible and intangible, with clearly defined side heads and subheads:

We come to you	RadioWeek
	Info-Pak
	Engineering Clearinghouse
	Employment Clearinghouse
	NAB National Campaigns

You can come to us	Research assistance
	Legal questions
	Technical inquiries
	General Broadcast Information
	electronic data search services

And you can meet broadcaster to broadcaster	National conventions, seminars, and meetings

Radio Awards bring recognition	NAB Crystal Radio Awards
	NAB's Distinguished Service Award
	NAB Broadcasting Hall of Fame

And special services bring discounts	Insurance Programs
	Publication discounts
	Long-Distance Service discounts
	Master Card with special benefits
	Promotional Items at low member prices

With so many benefits available, who would not be interested in membership? Page four reiterates the basic issues from the first page, then provides incentives for joining immediately. In addition to receiving regular benefits, those who join immediately will receive a New Member Kit "with News Vehicle and personal ID press passes, member decals, "NAB Tour" cassette, coupons worth $50 to $100 off upcoming seminar registration fees . . ."

The letter is signed by the NAB vice president, radio membership, rather than the president or senior vice president/radio, enabling the association to deliver a hard-hitting solicitation without criticism, since broadcasters expect the membership director to extol NAB's membership benefits in the most positive manner.

The postscript is a final offer with impact: "If you join by March 15, you can attend NAB '90 in Atlanta for just $100, a $375 savings off the $475 non-members' fee." Because the annual convention is extremely popular with broadcasters interested in seeing the very latest in equipment, each other, and the entertainment, the postscript is a tremendous incentive to join within the next 30 days.

The newsletter-style letter is printed in two colors: red logo, side heads, subheads, underlining, and P.S., and black typewriter type, printed on white paper.

The accompanying brochure, *AM Radio Update*, is informational rather than promotional in tone and is keyed to the primary interests of AM radio station owners and managers. Printed in two colors on an 8½" × 11" sheet of paper folded into six panels, the green topic headings are:

Programming
Listenership
Legislative Agenda
Daytimer Interests
Recent Studies
NRSC-1 & NRSC-2 Technical Standards
Antenna Design Projects
AM Band Expansion
New Certification Mark

Except for a standard self-addressed, postage-paid reply envelope, the mailing has only one additional piece—the NAB Radio membership application form. Unlike the AAA solicitation, the NAB brochure, membership form, and reply envelope contain no promotional offers or incentives. The complete display of membership benefits, special offers, and sense of urgency are conveyed exclusively by the four-page "newsletter," which is individually addressed. And the mailing is sent first class.

Monthly dues payments are a definite advantage in getting new members and renewing current ones. Rather than be required to pay out a large lump sum each year, members are simply asked to "recertify" the proper dues bracket annually. Because recertification is based on the past year's revenue, station dues are frequently lowered instead of increased, considering the volatility and intense competition of the radio industry.

The direct mail efforts alone produce substantial numbers of new members within the first few weeks after the mailings. Those who have not replied within a month are called by the telemarketing team.

There are variations on the NAB approach to new membership mailings for trade associations. Instead of a detailed cover letter with a low-key, informative brochure, some use a single-page letter with a colorful promotional brochure that depicts all the benefits plus special offers. These brochures, 11″ × 17″ folded into eight panels, also provide for two panels with built-in membership application forms for regular and associate members.

Exclusive Mailings. The Pepperdine University campus is built into the mountainside overlooking Malibu, California, and the Pacific Ocean. Affiliated with, but not owned by, the Church of Christ, Pepperdine is barely more than 50 years old. Originally it was located in a working-class neighborhood near downtown Los Angeles, then 20 years ago it moved its main campus to Malibu.

Although the university has nearly 40,000 alumni, only 5,000 to 6,000 are university donors. Many of the older alumni who graduated from the downtown college find it difficult to identify with the rich trappings of an oceanside campus near the film colony residents of Malibu. A large percentage of students were and still are from families who could not afford to send their deserving children to college, and have been or are subsidized by Pepperdine's generous scholarship programs.

In the past five years, however, the percent of alumni who are donors has nearly tripled from 4 to 11 percent, thanks to a thoughtful, carefully tested series of direct mail campaigns.

Originally, letters were sent to alumni inviting them to become "club" members—Century Club (up to $100 annually), Silver Century Club (up to $300), and Gold Century Club (up to $500 annually). The cover letter was addressed, "Dear Alumni."

That was followed by a test mailing of 24,000 that included 12,000 "Dear Alumni" salutations and 12,000 individually addressed letters with a personalized first name. The latter provided three times the dollar amount of the impersonal letters.

One of the most successful mailings was personalized even more. The cover letter included the date and amount of the last donation, even though it might have been made years earlier. Naturally, this works only with previous donors.

Constant experimenting continues to produce more favorable results. A "lost friend" campaign is based on the needs of the alumni, rather than the university. Outside the envelope a headline reads, "How Pepperdine can put you back in touch with a 'lost' classmate or friend . . ."

The entire package contains a single-sheet cover letter with typewritten copy on both sides, a FIND A "LOST" FRIEND reply card, a club membership form, and a postage-paid reply envelope—all in black and white.

Modest as this appears, the cover letter is extremely appealing in touching the needs of its alumni. The introductory sentence reads:

Where are the friends you studied with, worried with, dreamed with, laughed and cried with?

After describing the importance of past friendships, the letter explores attempts to strengthen the bonds of Pepperdine's alumni:

One way to do that, I believe, is to learn about your interests and needs, and for the University to try to fulfill them. We've learned from recent survey and census forms that Pepperdine College alumni enjoy reading about fellow alumni more than anything else in our publications. And many say they're very interested in communicating with other alumni, but often can't attend alumni functions because of distance, age, or other commitments.

That's why I'm enclosing a "Find a 'Lost' Friend" card for you. If you'd like to get back in touch with a "lost" classmate or friend, just fill in the card. All we need is the person's name and school.

Write your personal message on the card (or attach a separate sheet for a longer message), and we will forward it to the designated person. By including your own name, address, and phone number, your "lost" friend will be able to contact you.

The letter continues by expressing the hope that the person will also join one of Pepperdine's annual giving clubs. Not everyone who returns the "lost friend" card becomes a donor, but the results are gratifying and the concept brings the alumni community into closer contact.

Experimenting continues. Instead of gift checklists starting with the smallest amount and progressing to $600 on the Alumni Annual Fund reply form, Pepperdine now leads off with the higher amounts, in some cases $100 rather than $50, in others $600. By staggering the choices the university reduces the tendency to check off the lowest amount listed on the left.

Dollar amounts also vary according to the past history of the donors. Those who have never donated are faced with a varied checklist ranging from $25 to $200. A donor who has given $2,000 in the past will find a choice of $2,000 to $6,000.

Mailings have increased from four to ten per year, with no one receiving more than five. Markets are being further segmented by school, by class agents, even by companies where many alumni are employed.

Each graduating class has a class agent. Each agent formerly wrote his or her own letter to classmates, but the results were poor. Now the basic letter is written at Pepperdine, and each class agent personalizes it. Dollar returns from this mailing have tripled since the change.

A local ARCO executive sent a letter to other Pepperdine alumni who work for ARCO, asking for contributions and club memberships. This was so successful the university is duplicating this method with other large companies in the Los Angeles area.

Effective direct mail can be tailored for every budget. Mass mailers such as AAA and AARP can afford to spend millions. The Los Angeles County Museum of Art has a healthy budget, but the money is spent wisely. The Saint Louis Zoo and NAB mailings are far more modest, but equally effective. And Pepperdine University has demonstrated that constant testing and considering the needs of its alumni are effective substitutes for expensive, four-color brochures.

Small trade associations with few potential member companies and substantial annual dues paid in a lump sum annually take an entirely different approach. Initial mailings are more informational and considerably more thorough than those numbering in the thousands.

The United States-China Business Council is an organization with fewer than 300 members, all U.S. companies doing—or contemplating doing—business in China. Most current members are in the Fortune 500, multinational corporations with interests all over the world. Although they can well afford the US-CBC dues, these companies are subject to innumerable membership and charitable solicitations from nonprofit organizations. They give careful consideration to most legitimate requests, but expect association memberships to be cost-effective.

Each year, the council's potential member list includes approximately 400 top and middle management executives from nearly 150 companies—presidents, international vice presidents, and those directly in charge of business in China. Since membership is a team decision in most of these companies, each team member is sent a complete package of materials along with a three-page cover letter from the US-China Business Council president.

The letter is individually addressed on the council's letterhead, which includes the names and company affiliations of the board of directors. In a straightforward manner the president outlines the problems and opportunities of doing business in China, and asks potential members to join the US-China Business Council, where they "will receive vital information, access, and identity."

Membership benefits are then described in detail:

INFORMATION . . .
   • China Market Intelligence [newsletter]
   • The China Business Review [magazine]
   • Special Reports
   • Industry Studies
   • Business Information Center [including] a computerized database

ACCESS . . .
   • . . . personalized contacts with U.S. and Chinese government officials . . .

- Forecast Meeting in January
- Annual Meeting [and] Seminar of US-China Economic Relations in June
- Council Committees
- Working Groups on Patents, Export Controls and Export Finance
- Roundtables

IDENTITY . . .
- The US-China Business Council blue and red seal, which . . . identifies your company as having high business standards and the full backing of the Council . . .

Specialized Business Services [available] on a fee-for-service basis . . .
1) Proprietary Research
2) Investment Planning Briefings
3) Personalized Strategy Sessions
4) Expatriate Orientations

The cover letter's concluding paragraphs summarize the council's leading benefit, "the most effective private sector channel to the Chinese leadership," and asks the potential member to study the enclosed materials, examine the membership form, and call if he or she has any questions. While the president asks recipients to join, there is no hype and no special offers or discounts. The whole tone of the letter strongly implies that this full-service organization, with its highly trained and educated staff, is ready to deliver.

In addition to the cover letter an impressive package of materials is enclosed inside a white folder emblazoned with the US-CBC blue and red seal. The folder contains:

- *The China Business Review* magazine
- *China Market Intelligence* newsletter
- General Information brochure
- Member Firms brochure
- Foreign Investment Trends analysis
- Specialized Business Services brochure
- Council Committees and Working Groups

- Investment Advisory Program
- Upcoming Events
- membership application form

The complete package with cover letter (but no reply envelope) is sent by first class mail. Although it does not call for a hasty decision, the weight and approach suggest the need for an ultimate decision; this is not the type of mailing to be discarded without thorough analysis and discussion. Personal telephone calls follow two to three weeks later, carefully tracing the path of each company's decision-making process.

The Adler Planetarium of Chicago is unusual in that it has a direct mail campaign for new members only once every three years.

Because its seating capacity is only 450, the planetarium's membership is limited to 4,500. The overall annual renewal rate is close to 70 percent, and its larger donors ($100 to $250) renew at the rate of 85 percent.

Even the planetarium's annual renewal effort is modest. On the outside envelope of its mail package it states, "DON'T BE LEFT IN THE DARK." Inside a black glossy card with a gold headline and reverse white type repeating the theme and listing the membership benefits. The back is blank. A gold-on-white membership renewal form summarizes the benefits for each type of member:

I WANT TO RENEW MY PLANETARIUM MEMBERSHIP!

MEMBERSHIP BENEFITS:

Individual: Free Sky Show tickets, 15% discount in Planetarium Store, discounts on classes, invitations to members events, quarterly Newsletter [$25].
Family: Same benefits as above for all members of a family (living in the same household) [$35].
Contributing: Same benefits as above PLUS 50% discount on classes, free Sky Shows for guests and voting rights in the Planetarium Corporation [$100].
Inner Circle: Same benefits as Contributing Membership PLUS invitations to exclusive, behind-the-scenes events at the Planetarium and field trips [$250].

There is no cover letter with this renewal mailing and the reply envelope is *not* postage-paid. Family members renew at a considerably higher rate than individual members, but the planetarium is so respected by families in Chicago and the surrounding area that renewals are not a problem.

The next major mailing for new members will be in spring 1992. Subscription lists of Chicago-area residents are rented from *Omni, Discover, Sky & Telescope,* and *Astronomy* magazines. In past mailings, the returns have varied from 1.5 to 1.8 percent. The lists perform well because they exclusively target people with obvious similar interests.

In-house List Mailings. Not to be overlooked are three important lists within the nonprofit organization, updated each year:

- former members who cancelled;
- nonmembers who subscribe to or purchase publications; and
- visitors and people who have called or written to request information.

Each group deserves mailings with cover letters attuned to its interests, even though the enclosures may be similar.

Members who cancelled in the past two or three years are excellent prospects. Changes in personnel, policies, or economic situation often make them susceptible to arguments for rejoining. Former members may have had second thoughts about cancelling, and simply need to be prodded.

Let them know what they have missed. Describe new problems, new issues, new concerns, and what is being done about them. Summarize the organization's activities during the past year—exhibits, special events, conventions, seminars, special reports, or lobbying—and describe any membership benefits that have been added. Then tell them how much they are needed, and what they will receive in return by rejoining.

Nonmembers who subscribe to an association magazine or order special reports, directories, and other publications are usually potential regular members or potential associate members. Their type of membership should be determined when compiling the list, for it affects the cover letter. Since these nonmembers are familiar with the association through its publications, ask if they are aware of its many other benefits. Describe the benefits in terms of their relative values to regular or associate members, using two separate letters.

Few nonprofit organizations systematically maintain a record of visitors or of phone calls and letters from nonmembers seeking information. But those willing to store this data will be rewarded. Compare it with a retail store; people who walk in the store are prospective buyers. Direct mail attempts to attract those who may be interested, the passersby. Consider how much more receptive people are who have already familiarized themselves with "the store" by visiting or requesting information.

They, too, deserve separate cover letters soliciting their membership. Thank them for their interest in the institution or association and explain the organization's many other activities and the information available to its members. Again, prospective associate members should receive a letter emphasizing their primary interests such as conventions, exhibits, industry information, and member directories—as opposed to potential regular members who may be more interested in issues and government relations activities.

Direct mail is the common thread of new-member solicitation efforts. Regardless of the number or types of members, or amount of dues, the great majority of nonprofit organizations use direct mail in some form.

Individual-member organizations with low annual dues rely on direct mail for most of their new members. As long as the cost per new-member remains reasonable, organizations believe they don't need to try any other methods. In most cases, the cost of following mass mailings with mass telephone calls to the most productive zip code areas is prohibitive.

Many small associations with a limited staff are in no position to follow up their mailings with other methods. They simply reuse the tried and true lists and test new lists. Those with a few thousand known potential members in a profession do not even need to test new lists; they have their own updated lists of people in their particular profession whom they solicit two or three times each year.

Most nonprofit organizations use *only* direct mail to solicit new members. Others, however, augment their direct mail with various combinations of telephone follow-ups, personal sales calls made from headquarters or by regional representatives, members soliciting members, advertising, and telemarketing.

Telephone Follow-up

The printed word, relayed via direct mail, explains membership benefits in great detail, and produces many new members without need for discussion.

Using the telephone is also an effective method of gaining new members, particularly when preceded by direct mail. People frequently delay membership decisions. Solicitations may be discarded, sit on recipients' desks for weeks, or forwarded to others in the company for their recommendation or approval.

Telephone follow-ups provide the opportunity for individual contact that may prompt favorable decisions, or enable the caller to trace the decision-making process when materials have been forwarded.

Let us return to the hypothetical computer security associations. The association with few membership benefits and low annual dues solicits prospective members by renting extensive lists of companies and addressing correspondence to the "security director." It does not attempt to identify prospects by name, and relies exclusively on direct mail for its new members.

The second computer security association offers many valuable benefits and a staff of specialists, and requires substantial annual dues. It tailors its own lists, starting with the top 50 banks, savings and loans, insurance companies, and multinational corporations. Calls are made to the CEOs' executive secretaries, who identify others in the company who might be involved in the decision to join, including the security directors and those specifically in charge of computer security. A mailing is sent to nearly 500 individuals in these 200 companies.

Three companies join within the first few weeks of the mailing. After one month the membership director initiates a series of follow-up calls to the remaining 197 companies.

The caller speaks first with the person directly in charge of computer security to be certain the material was received and read. If the mailing was not received or was overlooked, another package is sent. If the person acknowledges reviewing the material, however, this line of questioning follows:

> What is your reaction to our organization? With the many confidential services we offer, don't you feel we can be of real value to you and your company?

This opens the conversation. The person may respond favorably, hesitantly, ask intelligent questions, or express reservations about the organization and its membership cost.

Though it is important to convey a positive response to all questions and remarks, it is equally necessary to trace the decision-making process and where it stands.

> Is this a decision that you alone can make or will others in the company be involved?

When the person claims to be in a position to make the decision, a substantive conversation follows and the caller asks the prospective member to join. But when others are involved, more information is required.

> Have they seen our materials? What is their reaction?

Quite often a co-conspiracy evolves, especially when the person in middle management wants to join, but someone higher in the company objects.

> What can I do to convince your management that membership in our association will more than pay for itself?

The telephone call may require a letter to answer questions or address the concern of the prospective member. In most cases, though, these individuals have all the materials they need to make the decision; they simply require more prodding.

There are two bromides that appear to refute each other. The first: "You will never make a sale if you don't ask for the order," and the retort, "If you have to have an answer now, the answer is NO!"

In selling nonprofit memberships by telephone, the truth lies somewhere in between. The prospective member must be asked to join, and though the decision cannot be forced, tenacity is the rule until a decision is reached.

For example, when told to call back in two weeks following a meeting when the proposed membership will be discussed, do just that. That conversation might proceed as follows:

Did you have the meeting where you discussed membership in our association? Did you decide to join? What are the problems? Is there anything I can do? When should I check back?

If the follow-up calls are delayed or not made, it indicates a definite lack of interest on the part of the organization. When calls are followed up on schedule, the original mailing takes on more significance. Even the company's top management will give membership more thought if they believe their company has been singled out as a desirable prospective member. The printed materials lose the stigma of a shotgun mailing when a company is pursued.

There is no reason to hesitate before calling company presidents and senior vice presidents when someone down the line says that the decision will be made upstairs. Most top management people are readily accessible when the subject is relevant.

Their secretaries can also be extremely helpful, particularly if they were instrumental initially in providing the names and if a telephone relationship has already been established. Frequently they are willing to divulge meetings held on the subject of membership, names of others in the organization who have been consulted, and the general status of the membership decision.

The telephone follow-up is worthwhile for most nonprofit organizations with a limited number of identified prospects, especially those with dues too high to warrant a quick response to direct mail. The telephone personalizes mail, provides prospective members with an opportunity to ask questions, and gently pushes them to make a decision.

Many potential members will arrive at a negative decision or an impasse, but if they are legitimate prospects, they should remain on the mailing list. Everything is subject to change, including the company's financial condition, regulatory or legislative concerns, the state of the general economy, or the decision makers themselves. The company may decide it should be a member after receiving the next mailing.

For those associations that use direct sales representatives, meetings that did not result in a decision should also be followed up by telephone calls. Personal meetings can be more effective than direct mail with meeting follow-up, but even then many prospective members are too tight to say yes and too polite to say no. They also require persistent prodding after the meetings. When confronted again they may loosen their purse strings or raise the courage to decline, but at least a decision will be made.

To the nonprofit selling new memberships, no decision is a "no" decision.

Telemarketing

The word "telemarketing" conveys the image of a boiler room operation with 50 or more people in cubicles telephoning numbers at random, reading a prepared script, pressing for the sale of an unwanted product.

Outside service bureaus develop leads by screening large lists. Cultural and educational institutions find them helpful in contacting university alumni or families in specific area codes. Many trade associations, however, are turning to in-house professionals to sell and service their members.

These telemarketing professionals are college-educated; have sales experience and pleasant personalities; and are motivated by good salaries, bonuses, and commissions. Telesales and teleservice people are normally career-oriented and in their late twenties or thirties. Teleprofessionals may be over 50, with years of marketing experience or knowledge of the industry and may be accepted as peers by the people they call.

While this approach exists, many nonprofits have refined the concept of telemarketing. They may engage outside service bureaus, hire in-house "telesales" people for aggressive new membership marketing, "teleservice" personnel to care for the needs of existing members, and "teleprofessionals" for top-level contacts, or use a combination of these options to increase their membership and nondues income.

Telemarketing has many applications in the nonprofit world. It is used to get new members, provide service to and renew current members, and reestablish contact with former members who have cancelled.

Organizations also have telemarketing operations that go far beyond membership sales and service: convention or special event registration sales, exhibit sales, market research, lobbying support, and fund raising, among others. Again, these activities are conducted both by outside service bureaus and in-house professionals.

The primary use for telemarketing by nonprofit organizations is, however, for membership. In general, associations that contact business and professional people in their offices use teleprofessionals, while nonprofits that call people at home contract with outside service bureaus.

As an example of in-house membership telemarketing, the National Association of Broadcasters Radio Division recently converted its membership sales operation from an outside regional sales staff to an in-house group of telemarketing representatives.

Its goals were clearly defined. NAB Radio budgeted for one teleservice and three telesales representatives to service its 4,000 member stations and sell approximately 6,000 nonmembers. Telemarketing activities were restricted to membership sales and service. Outside service bureaus would continue to be used for market research and efforts other than radio membership.

To install a new telemarketing facility, advance planning was crucial. Telephone and computer arrangements were made months before the target dates. Modular office systems required six to ten weeks notice prior to delivery. Advertising, interviewing, hiring, and training personnel took two months.

Working with the association's computer and telephone personnel, the telephone system provider, and the long-distance carrier representative, the membership director could examine workable alternatives, estimate telephone expenses, and secure discounts on computer hardware, along with advice on suitable software.

Decisions were made for handling inbound and outbound telephone traffic and the use of "800" numbers and WATS lines. A major decision was made to use a computer software program equipped with automatic dialing capabilities. This approach had several advantages.

- The general manager or owner's name, station call letters, address, and telephone number for every radio station in the U.S. would be stored.
- Every account activity would be stored in one place for each station, including summaries of conversations.
- All stations would remain active prospects because a specific follow-up action had to be stored in the computer before leaving the account.
- All telestaff members would have access to information on each station.
- Automatic dialing permits more calls and assures more accurate dialing.
- The use of computers reduces paperwork.

A computer was ordered for everyone in the membership department, including the telemarketing supervisor and membership director. A laserjet printer was installed to provide high speed, letter-quality correspondence to members and desktop publishing. It not only accommodates more staff members' needs than a regular printer, its fine quality printing enables its products to be used outside the organization.

NAB Radio also ordered four modular offices, large enough for privacy while allowing for close interaction and team spirit among the sales and support staff members. Modular systems are flexible; they can easily be arranged to accommodate additional units.

Display ads were placed in the *Washington Post* and broadcasting trade magazines to ensure a variety of telemarketing candidates. Resumes were requested, and face-to-face interviews were held only after at least three lengthy telephone interviews at different times of the day and evening with each candidate.

First priority was given to hiring people with broadcast industry experience, but some sales experience, a good personality, and the ability to close a sale were also important factors. Three telesales and one teleservice representative were hired, not all with backgrounds in broadcasting. Those in telesales received salaries of $28,000. As further incentive, the person producing the highest sales each month would receive a $1,000 bonus. The teleservice rep, who was hired to be particularly sensitive to the needs of current members, received $35,000 annually, with no additional incentives.

The operation is working well. To date, there has been no turnover; even the monthly bonuses are balancing out among the sales achievers.

Potential and actual member stations are divided into three regions, according to time zones. The Eastern telesales person works from 9 A.M. to 5 P.M., the Central rep from 10 A.M. to 6 P.M., and the Rocky Mountain and Pacific zones are covered between 11 A.M. and 7 P.M.

Once the system was in place, member stations were called. The ostensible reason for the first telemarketing call announcing the availability of a new "800" number for members with questions or problems. It was also an opportunity to explain the new telemarketing operation. Teleservice is a very effective means of retaining members. Now members can call a single number for legal, technical, or general questions related to broadcasting. While the representative knows few of the answers, he or she can refer members to the proper person.

Prospective members are called after direct mail campaigns. New-member efforts are also tied in with the two major annual conventions. By joining NAB prior to a convention, radio stations can save several hundred dollars in registration fees.

Former members are also contacted on a regular basis. Stations experience frequent personnel changes, and swings in the economy or in local ratings make unprofitable stations suddenly profitable again.

With everything on computer, each day begins with the callback file. Station by station, the telesales person can review past conversations and actions, then touch a button which automatically dials the station's number.

Special information, such as names of those who have attended past conventions and people who have called with problems or complaints, is on file for each station. This type of information is helpful in sales.

Membership sales have improved dramatically since the telemarketing operation was installed. The key to its success is the personal aspect and professionalism of its representatives. Both members and nonmembers identify NAB with a single person who can answer their questions.

Outside service bureaus also assist in membership campaigns. The Los Angeles County Museum of Art contracts with an outside tele-marketing service to supplement its direct mail membership drives. The ten experienced operators visit the museum periodically to tour the exhibits, read the promotion pieces, and receive training to answer questions or respond to complaints.

Although the operators read a prepared script when contacting the general public, their careful training by the museum staff enables them to depart from the script to answer questions or address objections.

Pepperdine University uses direct mail with alumni who have donated at least once to its alumni association, but it uses an outside telemarketing service bureau to contact those who have never given. Telemarketing is used for sales and screening. Those who give as a result are transferred to direct mail lists, and those who have questions or express interest are turned over to the Pepperdine staff for follow-up.

Telemarketing by an outside bureau also makes sense when every family in the metropolitan area is eligible to join. Direct mail has targeted lists, but there is a place for personal contact by phone.

Many nonprofits use telemarketing service bureaus for qualifying large number of prospective members. When there is genuine interest, but the questions are too technical or require professional assistance, the names and numbers can be turned over to staff members for follow-through.

Consider the three telephone methods for increasing membership sales: 1) telesales, with well-trained and well-paid achievers in-house; 2) teleprofessionals, experienced pros accepted as peers by prospective members; and 3) outside service bureaus for contacting the general public or for screening purposes. Only the in-house telesales operation calls for a major investment. Service bureaus are contracted by the hour, and teleprofessionals do not require computers.

Personal Contact

Making personal calls on prospective members can be extremely beneficial to an association, although it is seldom the most efficient approach. Personal calls provide instant feedback and help the organization adjust quickly to the mood of the times.

Personal calls are usually made by staff members from the headquarters' membership department, by other staff members from headquarters, or by regional sales and service representatives who live in the regions.

Membership Staff. The executive committee of a small association vowed to double its membership in three years. The committee hired a new vice president for development on a salary-plus-commission basis with the agreement that he would devise a marketing plan and implement it with no assistance other than a shared secretary.

The plan was not complicated.

- Three direct mailings per year to all potential owners and managers.
- Personal sales calls one full week each month, concentrating on group owners with six or more outlets.
- Correspondence and telephone follow-ups to meetings when not traveling.
- An equal amount of money budgeted for direct mail and travel.
- Cost-per-new-member results to be analyzed and methods compared annually.

The headquarters locations of group owners were broken down by state, then plotted on a large map of the U.S. Clusters of group owners by state and metropolitan areas were noted and ranked. Trips were planned 12 months in advance to states with the highest concentration of group owners, to have the greatest impact on membership growth.

Two weeks prior to each trip letters were addressed to the group owners in that state, advising them that they would be called the following week to arrange an appointment. Since they averaged ten outlets per group, and each outlet was considered a potential member, five group appointments in one week represented a potential of 50 new members. Dues were paid by the group, individual outlets, or both, but most required the approval of the group owner or president.

After securing at least five group head appointments in a particular week, the development vice president, with map in hand, called individual owners for appointments to fill out the week between group locations. In most cases, an additional ten appointments were made in advance, raising the week's potential new members from 50 to 60. In a five-day period, 15 appointments were scheduled, a manageable average of three per day.

On Sunday evening or early Monday morning the association V.P. flew to the airport closest to his first appointment and rented a car that could be dropped at the final destination.

Most potential members were delighted to meet with someone from the association's headquarters. They were anxious to discuss industry issues, problems with government regulatory agencies, and potentially damaging proposed legislation. The meetings, originally designed to be sales meetings, were actually a two-way exchange of ideas along with a discussion of the association's membership benefits.

For the first two years the direct sales contact program was a resounding success. An average of ten outlets joined during one week on the road. After telephone follow-ups to those that deferred a decision, an average of 14 new members were signed as the result of a single trip that first year, or 23 percent of the week's average 60-outlet potential.

By bringing in prestigious groups as new members, the association had generated a bandwagon effect, which was exploited in each successive mailing to potential members.

"Growth in Numbers and Influence" was a headline featured and documented with regularity in new membership brochures and the association's newsletter. The aura of "growth" was not only a stimulus in attaining new members, it carried over to old members as a strong incentive to retain their memberships.

For three successive years more than 400 new members joined each year, doubling the association's total membership as originally planned. Each year following the annual convention, a tabloid was mailed to both current and potential members listing the 400-plus new members that had joined in the previous 12-month period, along with pictorial highlights of the convention.

In that three-year period, direct mail and direct contact sales results were nearly equal. Year-by-year analysis of the two solicitation methods, however, revealed startling differences.

In the first year, personal sales calls outpulled direct mail. Because the association V.P. traveled to those states with the highest concentration of group headquarters, the potential number of members per call was very high.

By the end of the second year, results from the two methods were comparable. Direct mail produced slightly more new members than in the previous year, perhaps because of the bandwagon effect, while personal calls declined somewhat. Group locations were farther apart; greater distances had to be traveled between the targeted appointments.

Direct mail continued to hold the third year, but results from travel fell off considerably. Although no trips were scheduled without advance appointments with at least one or two group owners, the potential number of new members called on per week dropped from 60 the first year to just over 25 the third year. Most group owners had been covered; the cost per new member obtained through direct contact soared.

The lesson is obvious. Travel can be productive only when the potential number of new members and added revenue is high. Had there been individual prospective members only, and no group owners, travel costs would have been prohibitive from the start. It would have been more cost-effective to use direct mail alone, or mail followed by telephone calls.

Other Staff and Volunteers. Direct calls on potential members are occasionally made by association staff from other departments than membership. They may be staff economists or government relations experts, and capable of discussing the very latest developments in the industry or legislative and regulatory concerns.

There are leaders in every industry or profession—companies and individuals whose association membership would attract and retain more members. They may be singled out and visited by staff members when traveling in the area. There are also deliberate, planned campaigns of matching staff experts with their interests or concerns.

For example, a small association with a substantial annual dues structure targets 25 companies, leaders in the industry. These companies are familiar with the association, and many of their managers have called for advice or contributed to special fund-raising efforts when emergency lobbying was required. Many of their middle management subscribe to the association magazine, and even attend the organization's seminars. But none of the companies has joined.

Solicitation letters, follow-up calls, and an attempt by the membership director to meet with them have all been met with friendly responses, but no results.

The association president, leading staff economist, and government relations director divided the 25 companies according to their known interests. The economist was assigned companies that had demonstrated an interest in industry information. Those that had supported recent lobbying efforts were relegated to the government relations director. The president chose the three companies where middle management wanted to join but were unable to persuade their CEOs. There was an obvious need for face-to-face meetings to demonstrate the importance of these companies to the association.

This strategy of top-level staff people meeting with targeted companies can be rewarding when the stakes are high. Dues from one new member should cover the travel costs. Several new members will result in considerable additional revenue while adding well-known industry leaders who can attract other new members. Good will is also generated among those in all the selected companies, whether or not they join at the time.

At the other extreme are staff members or volunteers who are in direct contact with large numbers of potential members daily. Everyone who visits a museum or zoo is a prospective member. Convincing these individuals to join on the spot may not appear to be practical, but can be worth the effort.

The Saint Louis Zoo has an attractive brochure available to all who stroll through the grounds. Along with a map and animal symbols depicting the various buildings, there are brief descriptions and color photos of animals and birds as well as a listing of special events, including the Zooline Railraod and animal show and feeding schedules. On the back of this ten-panel brochure is a membership form to join the Saint Louis Zoo Friends Association.

Over the years a few families would take the brochure home with them, and later mail in a membership check. By adding a Saint Louis Friends Information Booth, however, the zoo currently signs up an average of 15 new members every day. Volunteers answer visitors' questions and actively solicit membership. The booth combines polite and friendly service with on-site sales.

The Los Angeles County Museum of Art has a more aggressive on-site membership sales program. Its nonmember visitors, unlike at the Saint Louis Zoo, must pay an admission fee. As they enter, nonmembers are presented an elaborate membership brochure which describes the many member benefits, including priorities and discounts.

There is an immediate incentive to join, since museum members are not required to pay an admission fee. By joining before they are admitted, they receive a substantial discount. An amazing 1.5 to 2.0 percent of all nonmember visitors join as they enter.

Those who do not join the same day are given a brochure that specifies the categories of membership as well as the privileges that are accorded each. The brochure includes a membership form; a self-addressed, postage-paid reply form; and a flap which can hold a check, for easy mailing.

The Pacific Whale Foundation, on the Hawaiian island of Maui, is a true believer in selling new memberships through direct contact with Maui visitors. The foundation owns a 50-foot motor vessel and a 50-foot sailing yacht at two marina locations; both of them boats available for whale watching. The foundation also owns a gift shop adjoining its offices.

By advertising heavily in local newspapers and magazines, PWF attracts hordes of visitors to its daily whale-watching tours. With the price of admission each person receives a "Complimentary Whale-watching Guide." This four-color brochure is extremely interesting and invaluable to whale watchers and other lovers of sea mammals. It describes the migration and distribution of humpback whales, their feeding habits, reproduction, identification, behavior, communication and song, and provides special tips for whale watching.

One panel of the brochure contains a membership form. On board ship, visitors are encouraged to join, and a large percentage of the foundation's 3,500 current members are the result of direct contact by PWF staff with tour visitors.

The Pacific Whale Foundation is unique in that it does not engage in any direct mail. All its members come from personal contact through tours and at the gift shop, along with some specialized magazine advertising.

Regional Representatives. Any number of large national nonprofit organizations have state associations in their field of interest. The state groups are engaged in lobbying their legislatures and working with state government regulatory agencies, as well as county commissions and municipal councils. Most have limited membership benefits, relying on the national organization for federal lobbying and national information concerning their industry, profession, or common interest.

Although the national organization is not directly competitive with the state entities, members must pay dues to both. Without some means of liaison, the national group may face attitudes ranging from apathy to resentment on the part of leaders at the state and local levels.

To offset this, many associations and societies employ regional representatives who live in the region and work on a salary-plus-commission or bonus basis. Each covers several states, mostly by automobile, attending state meetings and conventions, calling on prospective new members, and attempting to reinstate members who have cancelled.

As ambassadors of goodwill, regional representatives provide an identity for the national organization. Since most have lived in their regions all their lives, they are uniquely capable of interpreting the mood and anxieties of the region to the national headquarters. In turn, they have the ability to sell national membership benefits in terms that relate directly to the region's interests and concerns. This is an ideal situation for a large organization, as long as the representatives are productive and increased costs of sustaining them are offset by a growing net number of members and net revenue. Salaries and benefits rise with longevity; travel expenses within the region, to the annual convention, and occasional meetings at the national headquarters also climb each year.

One or two representatives with lagging sales can be retired or replaced, but what can the organization do when the regional representation system in general becomes a drain on its annual budget? There are three alternatives:

1. Consolidate the regions, reducing the number of representatives from eight or ten to four or five.
2. Eliminate the regional concept and bring in the top-producing

two or three representatives to the home office as national membership sales personnel.

3. Replace all direct salespeople in the regions with a telemarketing operation at national headquarters.

That is a tough decision not easily made. It requires more than a cost/benefit analysis. How important is the goodwill generated at the local level? Are gains in membership dues revenue outpacing inflationary rises in expenses? Is the total membership showing a net increase (old members plus new members minus cancellations) year after year? What are the three-year projections for the alternative methods?

The regional representative method might be compared with those using direct mail only: "If it works, don't fix it." Not all methods continue to be efficient year after year, however. When a particular method is no longer effective, supplement it or find the best alternative.

Members Soliciting Members

Individual professional organizations and societies have been successful in enlisting their members to help gain new members. With new member contests, participating members are rewarded with prizes and recognition. Member-to-member campaigns also create a new awareness of the association's many benefits, reinforcing current members' reasons for joining and strengthening the member retention rate.

The Radio-Television News Directors Association (RTNDA) is an organization of individual voting members and corporate supporting members, consisting of four membership categories:

1. Active Members (news directors and producers),
2. Associate Members (other electronic news staff),
3. Supporting Members (networks, TV and radio groups), and
4. Participating Members (broadcast equipment manufacturers and suppliers).

Before undertaking a new series of direct mail solicitations, the RTNDA board was in search of a means to generate some excitement and a sense of momentum.

They decided to launch a two-city campaign in New York and Washington where their present members would be asked to recruit nationally recognized radio and television network news personalities.

A list was compiled with the aid of the networks. The RTNDA president wrote to each personality, explaining what the organization was doing for electronic journalism, and how the membership could inspire other broadcast news people to join and work together, accepting the responsibilities that go with being "America's first choice for news."

Since most of the network broadcasters were located in New York and Washington, RTNDA also wrote to each of its active news director members in the two cities, asking them to contact personally the leading air personalities whom they knew.

It was explained to members this was to be the kickoff of a national effort to increase RTNDA membership among newspeople who were still unaware of the association. By recruiting nationally known broadcasters up front, they could help create the necessary momentum needed for the sustained direct mail campaigns to follow.

As an inducement, New York and Washington members would be credited in RTNDA's monthly magazine, *Communicator*, with their photos and photos of each new personality who joined as a result of their efforts.

When this word-of-mouth kickoff was determined to be moderately successful, it was decided to extend it to a nationwide campaign of "members soliciting members."

Through its newsletter, *Intercom*, and accompanied with a flier, RTNDA asked all of its members to recruit new members. The magazine did not describe the membership campaign; it reported the results. Each new member and the person responsible was mentioned in the *Communicator*.

As an added enticement, each RTNDA member responsible for signing five or more members during the year would be given special recognition at the December Annual Convention.

By itself the members-soliciting-members campaign was not a major factor, but as part of a coordinated effort with heavy use of direct mail throughout the year it added a sense of camaraderie. Members were being asked to participate, and they responded with enthusiasm. The direct mail effort was extremely successful, and as RTNDA announced the steady flow of new members, the old members knew they were an important ingredient in the total effort.

This campaign was practically cost-free, since it relied on quarterly articles in the newsletter to sustain the program, and monthly mentions of new members and their sponsors in the magazine.

Another association recently developed a low-cost member-soliciting-member campaign at its annual convention. In a heavily trafficked members' lounge area where members were free to call their offices and discuss business with other members, the association's membership staff handed out lapel flowers. They also offered to mail a postcard with a photo of the convention city to anyone of their choosing, provided they would also sign a postcard to a nonmember back home, a "wish you were here to enjoy this city and this convention."

Not only did this effort draw a favorable response, this member-soliciting-member test elicited the names of more than 900 potential members. The association provided a computer printout of the company names and addresses, but the members added the key ingredient—individual names within those companies.

Upgrading other members is another successful method of using members. Most cultural institutions have several levels of membership. Regular members are at the lowest rung of the social ladder.

The Los Angeles County Museum of Art has the typical range of membership levels from $55 to $1,500: Active ($55); Contributing ($90); Patron ($150); Sponsoring ($350); Supporting ($700); and President's Circle ($1,500). Each level up the ladder brings additional priorities and rewards.

The ultimate is to become a member of the exclusive President's Circle Patrons ($5,000). The museum enlists "Member Referrals" to recommend those who might enjoy becoming a member of the President's Circle or President's Circle Patrons.

Those recommended for membership in the President's Circle receive a letter from the head of museum membership, which includes this personal paragraph:

One of our members, [name of member] has suggested that you might enjoy becoming a member of that special group [President's Circle]. Our members receive a host of exclusive benefits designed especially for them by the Board of Trustees in appreciation for their generous patronage of the Museum. These benefits include:

* Invitations to black-tie "First Night" Preview Receptions for major exhibitions;
* Invitation to the Annual President's Circle Gala;
* Three free Museum catalogues annually and the handsome Museum Engagement Calendar;
* VIP ticketing privileges, personal handling of special exhibition ticket requests, and other services through your President's Circle Coordinator; and
* Much more.

Beneath the signature are the names of the friend who made the referral and the President's Circle coordinator, indicating that they have received copies of this letter of invitation. Few recipients would have the temerity to discard this mailing without serious consideration.

The accompanying brochure is elegant. The cover depicts a silver dish designed in 1742 on a deep forest green background with white lettering that states simply, "Los Angeles County Museum of Art President's Circle." Inside, the copy describes the museum and membership privileges for the President's Circle and President's Circle Patrons.

A flap inside the far right panel contains four white enclosures with green type that stands out against the forest green background. The first enclosure lists the Spring–Summer Event Schedule for President's Circle and President's Circle Patrons. Of the seven listed events, three are marked with an asterisk as "events exclusive to President's Circle Patrons."

The second enclosure is a membership form for President's Circle or President's Circle Patrons. Even with amounts as large as $1,500 or $5,000 prospective members are provided the opportunity to charge membership to Visa, Master Card, or American Express. There is also a blank for additional contributions to the Los Angeles County Museum of Art, as well as for gift memberships.

The third enclosure is a Member Referral card. The person who has been referred is now asked to refer others for membership in the President's Circle. It is doubtful that anyone not choosing to join would refer others, but it is a subtle reminder of the social privilege of being in a position to recommend friends to this prestigious group.

The final enclosure is a postage-paid reply envelope addressed to "The President's Circle, Los Angeles County Museum of Art."

There are countless methods of upgrading memberships, but using members to refer members is one of the most effective.

Other individual member nonprofits have contests that offer major prizes to members who solicit the most new members. New cars, vacation trips, and free transportation to the annual convention can be major incentives for members to participate. While these contests require much more publicity and the prizes (unless sponsored) add to the cost, they do produce results.

Trade associations often take a low-key approach. The board of directors may assign itself five or six prominent potential member companies to target for membership. Each board member identifies companies that may be located in his geographical area, or where the director has a close personal relationship with executives in those companies, regardless of location. While this may not result in significant numbers of new members, those companies that do join are influential and add to the strength of the association.

On a somewhat broader scale, many associations have an active membership committee that supervises a member-soliciting-member campaign. In one association where the directors are elected by members in their regions, this has been especially effective.

One of the directors is selected as membership committee chairman. The other directors suggest one member from each state in their region to serve on the membership committee, and the chairman appoints members from each state in his region.

The membership committee chairman, with backing from the other directors, coordinates the 50-person committee program. The association staff membership department provides a state-by-state breakdown of potential members, with names, addresses, and phone numbers, to the membership committee.

This type of campaign can be highly successful. Prospective members are contacted by their peers within the same state. There is time-consuming involvement by the committee members; they are on the political ladder in future board elections, since they were appointed by directors from their regions.

By enlisting directors and membership committees for member-soliciting-member campaigns, the association's membership staff is free to continue with the mundane, but consistent, direct mail and telephone efforts while its members are out beating the drums. It works, and there is member involvement.

Direct mail is another means of asking members to solicit other members, and is frequently used by nonprofit organizations with direct-mail-only member campaigns.

Stuffers with the newsletters or other mailings ask members to recommend other potential members. This is especially helpful to individual member organizations where it is difficult to identify others with common interests or concerns.

Others use this device not only with regular members; they ask potential members to identify other prospective members as well. In a recent mailing by the National Alliance of Senior Citizens (NASC), the reverse side of the Membership Acceptance Form carries the headline, "Nominate A Friend or Relative To the NASC!" It reads:

> If you would like your friends or relatives to learn how they can be nominated to Membership in the *National Alliance of Senior Citizens*, just fill in their names and addresses below and we'll send them materials with no obligation whatsoever. They'll be glad you did!

Whether or not the recipients joined the NASC, their lists of additional names and addresses would be extremely useful to the association in identifying other prospective members.

Membership Advertising

With ingenuity, membership organizations of any size are in a position to advertise for new members: free, paid, or trade.

Most association newsletters are sent to members only. Unless they are also read by nonmembers, there is no reason to advertise in them. Magazines and special reports that are sold to nonmembers, however, should carry some form of membership advertising in every issue and report.

House ads can be prepared in advance in all sizes and for all situations. One-third-page, half-page, two-thirds-page and full-page ads should be made available to the association's magazine editor for placement in each issue, according to the space available. The ads should contain a toll-free 800 number and a coupon if appealing to individuals who can make an immediate decision, and a fax number for potential corporate members to request additional information.

Special reports should carry a full-page description of membership benefits at the end of the report, preferably inside the back cover, asking the readers to write, call, or fax to request more information.

If the dues schedules are not too confusing, they can be included in the ads, but if they are complicated or expensive, it may be wiser to wait until the dues can be explained along with a complete membership benefits package to respond to requests for additional information.

Frequently associations with magazines in related fields are willing to exchange advertising, or at least agree to a 50 percent reciprocal discount off the published rates. For example, an association of chemical engineers might arrange to exchange advertising with other engineering association publications, or a retired military organization might exchange with military service association magazines.

Small, local public interest groups where the members have much in common could arrive at agreements to exchange small ads in their newsletters on a reciprocal basis. Since their members have common interests, the organizations could be strengthened politically and financially.

Large individual member associations use paid advertising for new members in both national and local magazines and newspapers. The American Association for Retired Persons, the Smithsonian Institution, the National Geographic Society, and the National Rifle Association, for example, advertise in selected commercial magazines and newspaper markets.

Before placing paid advertising in commercial magazines or newspapers, ask for a publisher's discount, which may range from 15 to 30 percent off the published rates. Test each publication with one or two advertisements, then measure the results. If a publication produces many inquiries or new memberships, but is barely above break-even, try a smaller ad. If the ads do not pay for themselves, drop that publication and try another.

The Pacific Whale Foundation advertises in Maui publications to attract visitors to its Whale Watching Tours and Gift Shop, but it also advertises in travel and education magazines that offer a free article in the same issue. The articles describe the migrations of humpback whales, research activities of the foundation, and their tours and Adopt-a-Whale program. The combination of articles and advertising produces many inquiries, memberships, and donations.

A few of the largest organizations that engage in mass mailings supplement them with local radio advertising. The American Automobile Association direct mail campaign described earlier arrived in January, at a time when motorists were most concerned with the need for towing or emergency assistance. Later in the month a local radio station carried a series of AAA commercials confirming motorists' worst fears, along with the benefits of joining at that time.

Radio advertising may sound extravagant, but if properly targeted, it is efficient. Radio stations provide detailed breakdowns of their listeners by time of day. AAA commercials were aired during commuter drive time, and were interwoven among news, weather, and frequent traffic reports. The station is highly rated, and its listeners are known to be responsive to dial-in numbers. In fact, the AAA radio campaign is undoubtedly successful without the direct mail. Combined, the results may be dynamic.

David Lawrence, the brilliant editor and founder of *U.S. News & World Report*, often explained to his staff, "There are ear people and there are eye people." There are those, he went on to say, who do not understand or believe the news until they hear it; others must see it in writing. Mr. Lawrence devoted a lifetime to informing Americans through the written word, charts, and graphs—the "eye" people.

Direct mail and print advertising are the nonprofit organization's most effective means of communicating with the "eye" people. Telephone follow-ups, telemarketing, and radio advertising appeal to the "ear" people. Personal sales calls combine the attributes of both, where the nonprofit staff representative speaks face-to-face with prospective members, and demonstrates and describes the organization's publications, special reports, and other benefits so they can both look and listen.

4. Analyzing the Results

At each year's end the membership department should analyze the results of retention and new-membership efforts, to determine the answers to these questions:

- How many old members renewed?
- Is the renewal rate rising or falling? Why?
- How many new members joined?
- How much did it cost to obtain each new member?
- If rented lists were tested, how did they compare?
- Was direct mail followed with telephone calls?
- Did the calls increase or lower the total cost per new member?
- Were personal sales calls being made?
- How do travel costs compare with direct mail costs, and what are the comparative costs per new member?

Retention Analysis

Assume an association sends its membership renewal notices every November for the next calendar year. In January, look back one year. How many members were there? How many old members cancelled or failed to renew? Do not include new members who joined during the past 12 months to determine the retention rate. Consider them separately. For example, if there were 1,730 members one year ago, and 292 failed to renew, the retention rate for old members is 83.1

percent. Compare that with previous years to determine whether there is a problem. If the rate varies within three percentage points, there is no reason for alarm unless it has been falling steadily each year. If the renewal rate takes a sudden plunge, the program should be reviewed.

Then look at new members who joined in the past year. What percentage of them renewed this year? How does that compare with old and new members the year before?

If the renewal rate for new members is significantly lower this year, there may be a flaw in the solicitation methods. Perhaps more benefits were promised than delivered. In certain regions, it may be the economy, which calls for an analysis of cancellations by region.

New Member Analysis

If the association rented or developed new lists of potential members, the test mailings should be compared. Figure 2-2 analyzes two test mailings to regular members, lists A and B, and two mailings to potential associate members, lists C and D. Annual dues for regular members was $120, for associates, $180.

List A produced 36 new regular members, compared to 27 for list B. By multiplying the annual dues by the number of new members, it

Figure 2-2. Analysis of Direct Mail Tests

New Member Mailings	Potential Regular Members Lists		Potential Associate Members Lists	
	A	B	C	D
Annual Dues	$120	$120	$180	$180
New Members	36	27	42	13
Gross Revenue	$4,320	$3,240	$7,560	$2,340
Printing & Mailing Costs	1,500	1,360	1,740	1,280
NET REVENUE	$2,820	$1,880	$5,820	$1,060
Cost per New member	$41.67	$50.37	$41.43	$98.46

was found that gross revenue achieved by list A was $4,320 and for list B, $3,240. When the printing and mailing costs were subtracted from the gross, the new revenue produced by list A was $2,820 and by list B, $1,880. Dividing the printing and mailing costs by the number of new members, it was found that list A cost $41.67 and list B cost $50.37 to produce each additional $120 in annual dues.

Differences in lists C and D were far more dramatic. The list C cost per new member was $41.43, compared to list D's $98.46, which was almost double.

There may be good reasons to continue mailing to all four lists, But A and C would certainly have priority. If these mailings of approximately 2,000 each were the results of testing much larger lists, it would be reasonable to exhaust complete mailings to lists A and C before turning to B and D. A and C would also be returned to more frequently.

Figure 2-3 examines the benefits of telephone follow-ups compared with the use of direct mail only. The small association with substantial annual dues and a liminted number of potential companies mails a solicitation package that produces nine new members with average annual dues of $4,735, or $42,615 gross revenue. After printing and

Figure 2-3. Direct Mail Only vs. Direct Mail with Telephone Follow-Ups

	Direct Mail Only	Telephone Follow-ups	Combined Methods
Average Annual Dues	$4,735	$5,370	$5,201
New Members	9	26	35
Gross Revenue	$42,615	$139,620	$182,035
Expenses:			
Direct Mail	12,771		12,771
Telephone & Time		18,324	18,324
Total	12,771	18,324	31,095
NET REVENUE	$29,844	$121,296	$150,940
Cost per New Member	$1,419	$704.77	$888.43

mailing costs the net revenue is $29,844 and the cost per new member is $1,419.

As a result of an intensive telephone follow-up effort to the mailing, an additional 26 companies joined the association, with average annual dues of $5,370 and gross revenue of $139,620. Since the mailing costs were already incurred, only telephone costs and the caller's time were considered, with net revenue of $121,296 and cost per new member added, $704.77.

This was a value-added analysis, not a comparison of direct mail with telephone, so the two efforts were combined for the net results.

Together, the mailing plus telephone follow-up produced 35 new members with average annual dues of $5,201 and $182,035 gross revenue. After total expenses the net membership revenue added was $150,940 and the cost per new member, $888.43. By adding the telephone follow-up, the cost per new member was lowered by 37.4 percent, or more than a third.

In figure 2-4, direct mail is compared with direct sales calls—where the representative travels from the association headquarters to meet with prospective members. Three mailings to the same list in one year produced 322 new members with average annual dues of $480, while the sales meetings resulted in 236 new members with average dues of $630. After mailing and travel expenses the net revenue was approximately the same ($133,210 for mail and $130,437 for direct sales).

Figure 2-4. Direct Mail vs. Direct Sales Contact

	Direct Mail	Direct Sales Calls
Average Annual Dues	$480	$630
New Members	322	236
Gross Revenue	$154,560	$148,680
Direct Mail & Travel Expenses	21,350	18,243
NET REVENUE	$133,210	$130,437
Cost per New Member	$66.30	$77.30

Even though sales calls cost more per member, the average annual dues produced was higher, balancing out the net dollar results.

Without a historical perspective, this would be most satisfying. Compare the past year's performance with the previous year, however, and the picture is disturbing (see figure 2-5).

Direct mail produced eight more members over the previous year, but average dues were down slightly, while expenses were up. The net

Figure 2-5. Direct Mail vs. Direct Sales Contact—1990 vs. 1989

	Direct Mail	Direct Sales Calls
New Members Produced		
1990	322	236
1989	314	271
	8	(35)
Average Annual Dues		
1990	$480	$630
1989	497	765
	($ 17)	($135)
Gross Revenue		
1990	$154,560	$148,680
1989	156,058	207,315
	($ 1,498)	($ 58,635)
Expenses		
1990	$21,350	$18,243
1989	18,827	16,081
	$ 2,523	$ 2,162
Net Revenue		
1990	$133,210	$130,437
1989	137,231	191,234
	($ 4,021)	($ 60,797)
Cost per New Member		
1990	$66.30	$77.30
1989	59.96	59.34
	$ 6.34	$17.96

revenue was off $4,021 and the cost per new member increased by $6.34. While not significant, this outcome bears watching.

The direct sales effort, however, is alarming. The number of new members declined by 35, average dues were off $135, and travel expenses were somewhat higher. As a result, net revenue dropped $60,797 below the previous year, and the cost per new member increased by $17.96.

In comparing the two methods, the cost per new member was almost identical two years before ($59.96 for direct mail and $59.34 for direct sales), but now direct sales cost $11 more per member than direct mail. Even though there was only a $3,000 difference in net revenues between the two methods, two years ago direct sales calls produced a $54,000 higher net than direct mail ($191,234 vs. $137,231).

Increased travel expenses were not the major factor, since direct mail expense increased approximately the same. Sales calls were being made on potential members whose dues would be lower on average and probably fewer calls were made per week. While it may not be possible to correct the situation, it should be watched closely during the coming year.

Thorough analysis of performance over the past two or three years is essential, and must precede the annual membership marketing plan. Analysis uncovers problems and successes, comparative costs per method, and changes in expenses. Armed with knowledge of past performance, the nonprofit organization membership director is prepared to devise a strategy for the coming year, then develop a detailed marketing plan with coordinated scheduling and realistic projections.

5. Annual Membership Marketing Plan

Even the smallest nonprofit organization should prepare an annual membership marketing plan. It is a self-imposed discipline that provides prescheduling of the promotional pieces to be printed, mailing lists to be rented, promotional letters to be written, telephone and/or direct sales calls to be made, and estimated budget for each.

Figures 2-6 through 2-10 demonstrate a direct mail campaign by the Radio-Television News Directors Association (RTNDA) over a 15-month period. Figures 2-6 through 2-9 detail the lists to be rented, mailing dates, and direct mail enclosures for each type of member—active, associate, supporting, and participating. Figure 2-10 coordinates the four campaigns in a single direct mail calendar with estimated mailout, expenses, and return for each.

Using rented lists from the National Research Bureau in Chicago, RTNDA first selected those titles in radio and television eligible for active membership: news directors, business and financial news directors, editorial directors and news producers, which were available by major metro and nonmetropolitan areas. Four mailings were to be sent to all titles in the TV and radio metro areas, and two mailings to the radio nonmetros.

The remaining National Research Bureau radio and TV titles were eligible for associate membership. They were also scheduled for mailings, with all TV and radio metro titles to receive two mailings and radio nonmetro one mailing.

Potential supporting members were scheduled for three mailings with lists taken from the *Broadcasting Yearbook*—radio and TV group

Figure 2-6. Active Membership Campaign

NATIONAL RESEARCH BUREAU LISTS:	POTENTIAL ACTIVE MEMBERS					
	Radio			Television		
	Metro	Non metro	Total	Metro	Non metro	Total
News directors	2,531	2,533	5,064	484	120	604
Bus. & fin. news directors	434	450	884	108	25	133
Editorial directors				136	21	157
News producers				32	8	40
TOTAL	2,965	2,983	5,948	760	174	934

SCHEDULE AND SAMPLES SELECTED FOR EACH MAILING:
January   all TV, all radio metro, half radio nonmetro
May   all TV, all radio metro, 2nd half radio nonmetro
October   all TV, all radio metro, 1st half radio nonmetro
January   all TV, all radio metro, 2nd half radio nonmetro

SOURCE LISTS:
National Research Bureau

DIRECT MAIL ENCLOSURES:
1. Letter from RTNDA president
2. Membership brochure
3. Active membership form
4. Postage-paid reply envelope (no. 9)

heads and network news organizations. Even though RTNDA is an association of individuals engaged in electronic journalism, the large companies owning groups of stations and the major news organizations are encouraged to join as supporting members. Many of these companies also pay dues for their news directors.

Potential participating members, the companies that sell news-related products and services to radio and television stations, were also scheduled for three mailings. Names were selected from lists of exhibitors and suite hosts attending other broadcasting association conventions and their lists of associate members, as well as those listed in the *Broadcasting Yearbook.*

The four new membership campaigns come together in the direct

Figure 2-7. Associate Membership Campaign

POTENTIAL ASSOCIATE MEMBERS

NATIONAL RESEARCH BUREAU LISTS:	Radio			Television		
	Metro	Non Metro	Total	Metro	Non Metro	Total
Anchorperson	4		4	72	76	148
News commentator				61	25	86
News reporter	454	467	921			
Sports manager	1,594	2,125	3,719	376	80	456
Sports editor				170	61	231
Sports producer				17	6	23
Sports announcer	301	303	604			
Weather director				185	52	237
Meteorologist				36	11	47
Women's interest editor/commentator	1,042	1,562	2,604	149	58	207
Public/community affairs	1,639	1,448	3,087	441	127	568
Public service	254	144	398			
Public relations	99	56	155	225	46	271
TOTAL	5,387	6,105	11,492	1,732	542	2,274

SCHEDULE AND SAMPLES SELECTED FOR EACH MAILING:

February All TV, half radio metro
June   2nd half radio metro, half radio nonmetro,
          except Women's interest commentators (¼)
October   All TV, lst half radio metro
February 2nd half radio metro, 2nd half radio nonmetro,
          except Public/community affairs (¼)

SOURCE LISTS:
National Research Bureau

DIRECT MAIL ENCLOSURES:
1. Letter from RTNDA president
2. Membership brochure
3. Associate membership form
4. Postage-paid reply envelope (no. 9)

Figure 2-8. Supporting Membership Campaign

SCHEDULED MAILINGS:
March   All
September All
March   All

SOURCE LISTS:
Broadcasting Yearbook—Radio & Television Group
Heads and Network News Organizations (approximately 600)

DIRECT MAIL ENCLOSURES:
1. Letter from RTNDA president (personally addressed)
2. List of current supporting members
3. Membership brochure
4. Supporting membership form reply card
5. Reply envelope (no. 9)

Figure 2-9. Participating Membership Campaign

SCHEDULED MAILINGS:
April   All
October All
March   All

SOURCE LISTS:
Approximately 400 selected news-related product and service companies
  from these lists:
• NAB Exhibitors & Hospitality Suite Hosts
• NAB *Associate Member Directory*
• Radio Convention Exhibitors & Hospitality Suite Hosts
• *Broadcasting Yearbook*

DIRECT MAIL ENCLOSURES:
1. Letter from RTNDA president
2. List of current participating members
3. RTNDA Members' Buyers Study
4. Participating membership form reply card
5. Reply envelope (no. 9)

Figure 2-10. Direct Mail Calendar—Estimated Mailout, Expenses, and Returns

		Mailout		Estimated Return		
		Number	Cost	Percent	Number	Annual $
January	ACTIVE	5,500	$ 2,750	.4%	22	$ 3,300
February	ASSOCIATE	5,000	2,500	1.5	75	3,375
March	SUPPORTING	600	600	1.0	6	3,000
April	PARTICIPATING	400	400	1.5	6	1,200
May	ACTIVE	5,500	2,750	.5	27*	4,050
June	ASSOCIATE	5,000	2,500	1.5	75	3,375
September	SUPPORTING	600	600	1.0	6	3,000
October	PARTICIPATING	400	400	2.0	8	1,600
	ACTIVE	5,500	2,750	.5	28*	4,200
	ASSOCIATE	5,000	2,500	1.8	90	4,050
January	ACTIVE	5,500	2,750	.4	22	3,300
February	ASSOCIATE	5,000	2,500	1.5	75	3,375
March	SUPPORTING	600	600	1.0	6	3,000
	PARTICIPATING	400	400	1.5	6	1,200
TOTAL		45,000	$24,000		452	$42,025

ACTIVE = $150
ASSOCIATE = $45
PARTICIPATING = $200
SUPPORTING = $500
*Numbers rounded from 27.5.

mail calendar (figure 2-10). A total mailing of 45,000 pieces was planned over the 15-month period, including every month except the July and August summer months and November and December when convention mailings were in progress. With each proposed mailing are the estimated mailout costs and estimated returns in numbers of new members and dues dollars expected. Not included are the estimated printing costs of the individual mailing enclosures.

An association that engages in telephone follow-ups would repeat the direct mail plan, adding a telephone schedule with calling periods, estimated telephone and time expenses, and the number of new members and revenue expected.

If an organization uses direct sales from the home office or the regions, another element is added. Each membership salesperson submits a schedule of trips planned and estimated number of new members to be signed. Based on this, travel costs and telephone follow-up costs for time spent when not traveling are determined. Each membership salesperson submits a schedule of planned trips for the year ahead and the estimated number of new members expected.

Unless the salesperson has a proven record of conservative estimates of new members expected, prudence suggests shaving 20 percent off the estimate so as not to be caught short at the end of the year. Most good salespeople are optimists, but in developing a marketing plan it is always safer to underestimate expected revenue and overestimate expenses.

Larger organizations that engage in radio advertising and/or telemarketing have more sophisticated means of coordinating their planned efforts. They have large staffs and computer assistance in staging various membership programs throughout the year. Their costs are also easily organized and estimated, based on computer-collected experience.

The basics, however, remain the same for new membership marketing plans in nonprofit organizations of all sizes (see figure 2-11). For direct mail efforts develop the lists, mailing pieces, and month-by-month mailing schedules, then estimate the net revenue after printing and mailing expenses. For telephone follow-ups decide which lists to call and the calling schedule, estimate new revenue added by telephone, less the costs of calling and time consumed.

In direct sales planning, decide who will be seen with a monthly

Figure 2-11. Elements of a New-Membership Marketing Plan

New Membership Schedules	*Estimated Costs & Returns*
Direct Mail	
Lists	Est. No. of New Members
Mailing pieces	Est. Gross Revenue
Mailing schedule	Less Expenses
	Est. Net New Revenue
Telephone Follow-Ups	
Lists	Est. No. of New Members
Calling schedule	Est. Gross Revenue
	Less Expenses
	Est. Net New Revenue
Direct Sales	
Lists	Est. No. of New Members
Travel schedule	Est. Gross Revenue
Telephone follow-up	Less Expenses
	Est. Net New Revenue

travel schedule, and when follow-ups will be made. Subtract the estimated costs of travel and phone calls from the estimated new gross revenue to determine new revenue expected.

Membership retention and renewal planning differs somewhat from new membership marketing. The entire program is scheduled and costs estimated, but no new revenue can be expected unless there is a dues increase. The only true gauge of effectiveness is the retention rate as compared with previous years and, of course, the renewal dollars received.

Plan the number of articles to be placed in the house newsletter and magazine (see figure 2-12). Will they appear monthly or quarterly? Who will write them? Although they add no expense, a schedule is helpful to the membership department and the editors to enable them to plan ahead.

What other informative means will be used to retain present members? Will there be quarterly reports or special letters from the

Figure 2-12. Elements of a Membership-Retention Plan

Membership Retention and Renewal Schedule	Estimated Expenses
Articles in association publications: Newsletter schedule Magazine schedule	
Quarterly Reports schedule	Printing & Mailing
Informative Telephone schedule	Telephone & Time
Annual Renewal: Renewal letter schedule Telephone Follow-ups schedule	Printing & Mailing Telephone & Time

president? Will the members be called at least once a year to offer additional service?

Finally, work into the schedule the timing for the annual renewal or recertification letter, and telephone follow-ups, if possible. After scheduling the combination of informative and sales retention and renewal efforts and estimating the expenses, the membership department will have a plan and a budget.

Membership marketing provides a financial base for nonprofit organizations that depend heavily on member dues. Retention and growth are measures of the critical political base for associations engaged in lobbying at the federal, state, and local levels.

Membership benefits must be understood if they are to be exploited properly. What are the tangible and intangible reasons for joining, as expressed by the members themselves? How do they differ by types of members? What are their common interests and concerns?

When the relative importance of benefits has been carefully analyzed, membership retention, renewal, and new membership campaigns can be planned. Depending on the size, dues, staff, and financial strength of the organization, various combinations of methods will be employed: direct mail, telephone follow-ups, telemarketing, direct sales, members soliciting members, and advertising can be interwoven.

Prior to developing a membership marketing plan, however, analyze last year's efforts. What was effective and what failed? How did each method compare with previous years? Did new membership and renewals rise more than expenses?

After adjustments are made as a result of the analysis, a detailed membership marketing plan is necessary for all those who will be involved. Accountants, editors, advertising people, telemarketers, and print coordinators who order printing should be aware of their role in the success of the membership campaign.

As Benjamin Franklin said, "Plan your work and work your plan." A thorough membership marketing plan can be implemented and coordinated without frequent crisis meetings, sporadic requests for additional budget approval, printing delays, or year-end surprises such as spending over budget and overestimated revenue.

Any plan is better than no plan. A marketing plan that has been thought through and spelled out for all concerned, however, should function smoothly and be on target.

III. NONDUES REVENUE MARKETING

Nonprofit management understands the fundamentals of maintaining a healthy membership dues base. As organizations develop, their members' needs surpass the original benefits covered by dues.

Most nonprofits other than educational, health, and cultural institutions were formed to meet a common cause or concern, local or national. They may have started with a newsletter and volunteers who organized a small group to protest pending legislation or to protect their common interests. As the organizations evolved, they hired an executive director and a staff secretary/assistant to manage the day-to-day operations and coordinate the work of the volunteers.

Today, associations and societies provide virtually unlimited services for their members and, frequently, nonmembers. Many services are not covered by dues; if they were, the dues would be prohibitive. Instead, members are offered a panoply of benefits, available to them usually at a discount.

The list of possible sources of income for nonprofits continues to grow, with innovations added yearly. Services and products are sold to members and associate members who sell or service regular members, and to nonmembers at a higher price.

While some products and services are available to nonmembers at a substantially higher cost, most are initiated by and for the membership.

Associations publish or distribute newsletters, magazines, directories, special reports, research studies, and books of interest to their members. They produce audiovisual materials for professional better-

Figure 3-1. Possible Sources of Nondues Income

Information Services
 Publications
  newsletters
  magazines
  directories
  special reports
  books
 Audiovisual Materials
 Computer Services
 Consulting Services

Advertising Sales
 Publications
  newsletters
  magazines
  directories

Meetings, Conventions, and Special Events
 Registration Sales
 Sponsorships

Exhibits and Suites

Financial, Travel, and Personal Services
 Insurance
 Bank Credit Cards
 Hotels, Airlines, and Car Rental Discounts
 Gift Shops and Promotional Items

Fund Raising

---

ment or entertainment. Computer services may consist of computerized databases developed by the association, or shared information databases and computer bulletin boards for an on-line interchange among members. Consulting services, specialized proprietary research studies, and employee training services are offered by some organizations, to their members on a fee basis.

Other major sources of nondues revenue such as advertising and exhibit sales are funded primarily by companies that sell products and services to association members.

Advertising can be sold by organizations of all sizes. If an association's publication is a newsletter, it may accept advertising. Magazines are obvious producers of advertising revenue, but other publications such as member directories and convention programs also have advertising potential.

Seminars, conventions, and special events are great revenue producers for nonprofit organizations. In addition to registration sales, luncheons and dinners can be sponsored to reduce their expense.

Expositions attract exhibitors, a major source of income, and even convention hotel suites can bring associations a surcharge from the hospitality suite hosts.

Financial services such as bank credit cards, credit unions, and insurance savings plans may be sponsored by nonprofits. Other services may include business insurance and travel services or discounts from airlines, hotels, car rental companies, or long distance telephone companies. Many organizations even sell members promotional items from sportswear to office accessories, when they are related to members' interests, or headquarters has gift shops for visitors.

There is another revenue producer more serious in nature, but frequently essential. Hospitals, museums, universities, and other institutions rely heavily on fund raising for capital projects, new equipment, and acquisitions. Associations, too, turn to fund raising when impending legislation or threatened regulatory changes create an atmosphere of crisis among their members. Such emergencies require additional funding, far more than is available through dues and ordinary nondues activities.

Fund raising for lobbying support can be accomplished in-house by staff members, although the money itself may be used to engage outside consultants or lobbyists on a temporary basis.

Even with nonprofits, income must exceed expenses, to fund the organization's activities.

6. Information Services

One of Dow Jones' most revered executives expounded on "The Dow Jones Theory." There was no transcript of the after-dinner-by-the-fireplace remarks, but they followed this line:

News is a commodity. As it comes in, news is a raw material, similar to wheat. It can be refined to flour, and turned into bread or cake. It can be packaged and repackaged.

Our reporters and correspondents bring us the raw news. Much of it is sent through our wire service to newspapers and businesses. We process the raw news and publish a daily newspaper, the *Wall Street Journal*. We refine it further and produce our respected weekly tabloid, *Barron's*.

Dow Jones carried the theory to its ultimate by attempting to publish the chaff through a weekly newspaper, the *National Observer*. The public was not ready for such an obscure approach to feature news at the time, but Gannett and Time Warner Inc. have proven the theory with today's popular newspaper, *USA Today* and *People* magazine.

Information is news with a long life span. It, too, is a commodity to be refined, packaged, and repackaged.

Publications

Newsletters, magazines and special reports are news when first released; they have a sense of urgency. Later, however, when articles and research studies are distilled and packaged by subject, they acquire historical informational value.

At year's end, magazine volumes can be sold with attractive binders, rather than disposing of the overage in storage. Reprints of articles and interviews remain popular when sorted and sold by subject matter.

The National League of Cities and United States Conference of Mayors, when they were colocated, packaged all of their publications and offered them to a new type of member, Research Associates. NLC's regular members consist of state municipal leagues and thousands of towns and cities of all sizes, while USCM's regular members are the mayors of medium size and major cities.

Neither group had nonvoting associate members, but each was frequently approached by companies and other organizations in the field of urban affairs interested in becoming affiliated with it.

A brochure—with this proposal—was mailed to these companies and associations:

The National League of Cities and the United States Conference of Mayors cordially invite organizations with an active interest in urban affairs or municipal marketing to become Charter Research Associates.

Public Affairs Directors and Marketing Directors in business and industry, government agencies and educational institutions as well as other associations concerned with the problems and improvements of our nation's cities, now have a unique opportunity to receive vital insights and up-to-the-minute evaluations from the two organizations that truly represent the interests of municipal government.

Although it was explained that Research Associates were not entitled to vote or hold office, they would receive all NLC and USCM publications, reports, research studies, urban affairs abstracts, and audio cassettes. If nonmembers purchased each of these items separately, they would pay $210 more than the annual dues for a "for profit," or, if they were nonprofits, they would pay $300 more.

Thus a new type of member was born. Information previously unsold or undistributed was disseminated to other organizations with a common interest or concern, additional revenue was added, and the new members were pleased to be plugged into and affiliated with two influential public interest groups.

Packaging publications is not the norm, but when circumstances are favorable, it is well worth consideration. The more popular approach is to devise a system for selling each of the publications or reports separately and through publications brochures, cross-promoting where possible.

Newsletters. Most nonprofit organizations do not charge members for their newsletters, the cost of which is included in the dues. There could be situations, however, when nonmembers might be willing to subscribe to newsletters at a premium in order to obtain information not otherwise available.

Take, for example, nonprofit newsletters for environmentalists or animal rights activists. It would be unseemly to accept their adversaries in business, industry, and the government as associate members, but why not sell them subscriptions to their newsletters? Instead of "selling out to the enemy," they would be performing a service.

If the lumber and chemical firms, the gun manufacturers, and the fur industry better understood the complaints and arguments of consumer activists as expressed in their newsletters, they might find ways to reach some understanding before facing the TV cameras and courtrooms.

Nonprofit organization bylaws may preclude membership of certain groups, but in most cases should not prevent the sale of publications, including newsletters, to all who have a common interest or concern, even though their viewpoints may be diametrically opposed. By setting a stiff nonmember rate, the nonprofit group gains additional nondues revenue, while the information is available to all who are sufficiently interested to pay the premium.

Magazines. Associations and institutions that publish magazines also send them to members as part of dues, in most cases. Universities such as Pepperdine and the University of California at Los Angeles publish slick quarterly magazines for students and alumni. *Pepperdine People* contains uplifting articles, with no advertising; *UCLA Maga-*

zine, with a much larger circulation, has both news and feature articles, interspersed with consumer advertising.

In some associations and societies the magazine is the primary inducement for joining. The Marine Corps Association, for example, offers new members a choice of receiving the *Marine Corps Gazette*, a monthly professional journal of interest primarily to Marine officers and top noncommissioned officers, or *Leatherneck*, a broad general interest monthly magazine for Marines and former Marines of all ranks. The National Geographic Society is another example—members often join to receive *National Geographic* magazine. Neither of these nonprofit organizations engages in lobbying activities; their primary purpose is publishing.

Some associations known for representing their members' interests through government relations efforts and providing industrywide information, however, publish magazines that are also of interest to non-members who are not in a position to join.

Many of these potential subscribers can be reached through the magazine itself. Every issue should contain an advertisement appealing to those who are reading a passed-along copy. One approach is to list major articles they may have missed, or articles set to appear in future issues.

Insert cards inside the magazine are particularly effective. They can be torn out, filled out, and mailed postage paid while the reader's interest is at a peak (see figure 3-2).

Advertising exchanges with other magazines is another practical means of finding new subscribers. Trade agreements are a way of life. Negotiate with editors or marketing directors of other nonprofit organizations with similar interests. They are just as concerned with broadening their circulation base. New subscribers not only add to revenue; they enable a magazine to increase its advertising page rate without raising its cost per thousand readers.

Since corporate memberships limit the number of copies sent to a single company as part of dues, offers should include a "member rate" and a "nonmember rate," where employees of company members are entitled to the member rate. If the association provides only three subscriptions per company member, and each copy is passed along to an average of ten people in the company, 27 potential subscribers within that company are eligible for the member rate.

Figure 3-2. Postage-paid Subscription Card

In addition to advertising in the magazine, trade associations can write to the company's representative member, offering a "group rate" for those employees interested in having their own copies. Frequently the company will pay for these subscriptions on top of dues if management believes the magazine is of sufficient value to the company's key people.

Those who write in for information from or about the association comprise another group of prospective subscribers. If eligible for membership, they receive membership solicitations; if not, offer them a magazine subscription at the nonmember rate.

Many nonprofit organizations send complimentary copies of their magazines to key people in Congress, pertinent government agencies, and other associations with similar concerns. Some also have a policy of providing free copies to key advertisers and advertising agencies.

If an association is not careful, however, complimentary copies can become an unnecessary drain on the budget. The complimentary mailing list should be screened annually. With the exception of those most essential to the association's vital interests, the remaining recipients should be sent a reminder of the organization's generosity, and the need to convert them to paid subscribers if they are to continue receiving the publication. Many (outside the advertising community) will subscribe because they have read a sufficient number of issues to be hooked as serious readers, and they are people with common interests.

When should a nonprofit magazine use large direct mailings to attract potential subscribers? Only when not in competition with the membership department. If membership dues are low, and the organization has individual rather than company members, sell the magazine only as one of many membership benefits.

For example, *Modern Maturity*, an excellent magazine, is published by the American Association of Retired Persons. Since annual dues are only $5, however, AARP advertising in the magazine sells the membership first, with the magazine as merely one of many benefits.

In the February–March 1991 issue of *Modern Maturity* is a full-page, four-color advertisement that leads off with the travel opportunities available to AARP members: tours, cruises, vacations, and discounts in air fares, car rentals, and hotel rates. The body of the ad also states:

Your $5 membership brings you other valuable benefits, too. They include . . . a subscription to Modern Maturity . . . free consumer and retirement planning publications . . . eligibility for AARP's Group Health Insurance Program . . . opportunity for auto and home insurance . . . the AARP VISA Card . . . savings on prescriptions through the AARP Pharmacy Service . . . and active representation of your interests in Washington.

The advertisement has a large clip-out coupon across the bottom, and a red, white, black, and blue insert card overlay, with two postage-paid tear-out reply cards for potential members.

The remainder of the insert card—which is at the back of the magazine—is also used as a tear-out reply card with the headline, "SIGN ME UP." It is opposite a two-thirds-page advertisement with the head, "IF YOU WAIT 'TIL RETIREMENT TO JOIN AARP, YOU'LL BE ABOUT 15 YEARS TOO LATE," and another large coupon across the bottom of the ad that says, "I Can't Wait. Sign Me Up Today."

Even the back cover of this issue, which features a major article to be covered in the next issue, repeats:

Membership brings you the AARP BULLETIN, MODERN MATURITY and a host of other quality services

In other words, if you really like the magazine, and want even more, join AARP. Since the annual dues for individuals are so low, it makes no sense to sell the magazine subscription by itself through advertising or direct mail.

Trade associations with a limited number of corporate members and relatively expensive annual dues might consider the merit of direct mail to groups of prospective subscribers. For example, associations in the chemical or petroleum industries may have relatively few member companies. Their magazines, however, may be of interest to chemical or petroleum engineers throughout the world. Why not rent lists of engineers to try to sell additional subscriptions? That would broaden the circulation base, add income, and increase the association's influence worldwide.

Libraries are another potential source of subscription revenue.

Public, university, and business libraries are worth testing. Magazines in libraries will attract many unknown readers who may be interested in becoming subscribers or, possibly, members. That alone would justify running both a subscription and membership ad in every issue.

The circulation manager is familiar with still another group interested in the magazine—subscription agencies. There are many reputable agencies with representatives in small outlets and newsstands all over the United States. For approximately 15 percent of the subscription rate, they will include an association magazine in their list of publications, and fill the orders that come in from their representatives. Subscription agencies are not to be ignored. Similar to libraries, they can uncover subscribers who might never appear on rented mailing lists.

As mentioned earlier, magazines can sell entire volumes with binders at the end of each year, or advertise the binders alone to readers who save their back issues.

Single issues and reprints of articles are frequently requested. There is seldom a justification for mailing them to nonmembers without a charge; at the very least postage and handling costs should be covered.

Every 12 to 18 months, major articles should be sorted by subject and packaged for resale. A magazine for veterans, for example, could break down its recent articles on military battles or events by World War II, Korea, Vietnam, and the War in the Gulf, then sell them to the veterans of each war. Advertising in the magazines, use of stuffers in members' mailings, and listings in a publications brochure should provide the necessary exposure as a reminder that these packaged reprints are available. The maxim, "Nothing should be left unsold" can be amended to say, "resold."

Directories. Membership directories are usually published only when of benefit to the association's members. Many professional organizations list their members because the members themselves are interested in contacting other members.

Some nonprofits have a policy of distributing their directories to members only; they do not want commercial enterprises to use these names as a direct mail or sales contact list. In those instances, additional revenue cannot be derived from the sale of their directories to nonmembers. Advertising can be sold to suppliers or associate members, however, because directories have a life of at least one year, and are frequently referred to by their customers.

If there is no policy against selling member directories to nonmembers, the price may be set so high that suppliers may be inclined to join as associate members, just to be eligible for other benefits. A membership directory is seldom advertised or sold by direct mail; it is more often used as an inducement to potential advertisers and prospective members.

In addition to directories of regular and associate members, associations may publish business directories related to their members' particular fields of interest.

The United States-China Business Council does not have associate members, but it does publish an annual *U.S.-China Business Services Directory*, which is sold at member and nonmember rates. This directory is extremely beneficial to companies frustrated in their attempts to do business in China, since it lists "more than 900 U.S., Hong Kong, and Chinese companies providing China business services, including consultants, agents, architectural and construction engineers, freight forwarders, attorneys, and more."

The principle behind nonprofit directories is their need to be of benefit to members, while adding nondues revenue through their sale, the sale of advertising, or both.

Special Reports. Developed in-house and often containing original association research, special reports are a dependable revenue source. Even though one copy may be sent gratis to members when first released, there are many potential buyers at both the member and nonmember rates. A well-documented report should have a life of approximately three years, a lengthy period in which to market it.

When published, the report deserves an article in the association's newsletter and magazine. At the end of each write-up, describe how to order the special report and include the member and nonmember rates.

In subsequent issues, run a large display ad with a coupon in the newsletter and magazine. Advertising reprints can also be used as stuffers in mailings to members. If the report justifies a price of more than $50 from nonmembers, it may be worth testing small paid ads with coupons and an 800 number in publications aimed at readers who have similar interests. The small advertisements can be used in the association's newsletter and magazine after several months of major advertising exposure.

If the report's subject matter is of interest to easily defined groups of nonmembers, test the mailing lists for direct mail sales. For example, an association for travel professionals releases a special report on travel to South America. It then tests a list of Americans who traveled to South America during the past 12 months. An nth-name mailing of 2,000 would cost very little, yet might produce a surprisingly large number of special report sales. If successful, the association could rent the remainder of the list.

Special reports will continue to produce income if nurtured through their life cycle—publicized when first released, advertised boldly in the house publications, fliers stuffed in mailings to members, advertised in other publications, offered to nonmembers through direct mail, and listed in the association's publications brochure for three years or until the report has been updated.

Books

Another rewarding source of income to nonprofit organizations is the sale of books to members. Nonmembers may also be invited to purchase the books, but at a much higher rate.

The American Society of Association Executives publishes an annual catalog of books and other publications. ASAE nearly doubles its book prices to nonmembers. With more than 21,000 association executives reading its publications, ASAE has a large following of prospective book purchasers.

The ASAE lists books and periodicals for sale by the following categories:

* Best Sellers
* Administration/Structure
* Associate Members
* Association Activities
* Association Law
* CEO/Volunteer

* Communications
* Conventions
* Education
* Finance/Taxes
* Government Affairs
* Human Resources
* Management
* Marketing
* Membership
* Other Resources
* Library Package/CAE

ASAE has books available on every conceivable subject of interest to association executives and department heads. Other associations can provide the same service for their members, but this is also true of individual member nonprofit organizations that center around hobbies or special interests.

There are books on golfing, fishing, and skydiving for sports enthusiasts; books on the environment for environmentalists; books written by and about Hispanics, Italians, Jews, and Poles for ethnic organizations.

The Marine Corps Association in Quantico, Virginia, has both a Bookservice Catalog and a spacious bookstore for Marines and former Marines who visit the Quantico Marine Base, known as the "Crossroads of the Marine Corps."

The MCA Bookservice purchases books from major publishers at a 40 percent discount (on average), 50 to 55 percent when they buy in volume, but only 20 percent from those publishers who know they have a hot property. They take nothing on consignment because of the paperwork involved.

The MCA Bookservice Catalog offers these book categories to its members:

* Marine
* Aviation
* Civil War
* Brotherhood of War Series
* Terrorism

* Other Wars
* Histories of Divisions
* World War II
* Korea
* Vietnam
* General Reading
* MCA Heritage Library Series
* Duncan and Moore
* Leadership—Reference
* Travel
* Reference
* New Arrivals

MCA promotes its books with stuffers in mailings to members, renewal notices, "Welcome Aboard" letters to new members, and "Dear Parent" letters to parents of new recruits who have recently joined the association. The catalog is sent with all orders and is free on request to all who write or call in.

Books are also heavily advertised in the association's two monthly magazines. Military people buy military books, particularly Marines. The Commandant of the Marine Corps has a recommended Leadership Reading List, frequently updated, for career Marines. The MCA Bookservice maintains all books on that list in stock for their members. All book prices are discounted for members; nonmembers must pay an approximate 20 percent surcharge.

A publications brochure is a must for every association, whether or not it sells books. The brochure or catalog is an enticement to potential members, and provides significant income from both members and nonmembers.

Brochures are included in most mailings to those who ask for information or inquire about the association. Inside, fully describe all publications and reports issued in the past three years—newsletters, magazines, special reports, research studies, and books that are still available. If the organization has audiovisual materials, include them. And don't overlook the order form—make it easy.

Audiovisuals

Audiovisual materials are an extension of publishing. Audiotapes, videotapes, and occasionally films are an added dimension to a nonprofit's publications services. They may be produced and sold as a · supplement to written training materials, or purely for their information or entertainment value.

It is common practice to record each of the individual panels and sessions at conventions and seminars, for resale to attendees as well as those interested but unable to attend. Taping services are available through the hotels and conference centers where events are held, if an organization does not have the equipment or know-how.

Attendees are encouraged to place their orders for audiotapes while at the meetings; the tapes are mailed to them later. Order forms can also be enclosed with newsletters published shortly after the meetings, while interest is still high, since the newsletter usually contains descriptions of the various sessions.

Videotapes are becoming increasingly popular with nonprofit organizations. For example, the National Association of Broadcasters offers the following:

NAB Videotapes	*Member Price*	*List Price*
MegaRate$: How To Get Top Dollar for Your Spots		
Book	$ 15	$ 30
Videotape (book included free with tape)	85	105
Radio America	29	75
Radio Is the Future	39	59
Radio Station Acquisition	249	349
Staying Out of the Libel Stew	60	100

The National Association of Chain Drug Stores (NACDS) has nearly 200 chain drug corporations as members, representing more than 21,000 retail pharmacies, and employing over 80,000 pharmacists and 450,000 personnel.

NACDS provides its members with a broad selection of training and educational audio and videotapes, and has films that may be borrowed or purchased:

Chain Drug Stores/An American Evolution: a documentary film that chronicles the growth of the industry.

The Right Choice: a film for high school and college students on educational preparation, career options, and job responsibilities as they relate to the profession of pharmacy.

RX for the Future: a film for pharmacists on how to encourage students to make pharmacy their career choice.

NACDS/Cornell Home Study Program on Chain Drug Store Management and Operations: for store employees; also provides ten credit hours of continuing education for pharmacists.

Trade associations have unlimited opportunities to provide audiovisual materials for members and their employees. Those under the age of 40 have been exposed to television all of their lives. Most of their news, information, and entertainment has come from TV rather than the printed word.

It is unthinkable today to attempt the training of new employees with printed training manuals unaccompanied by audio or visual materials, preferably the latter. Information, too, can hardly be absorbed without sound and visual dramatization.

A few associations, such as NACDS, publish impressive annual reports with the past year's accomplishments, activities, and services provided by the organization. A videotaped annual report might also have several advantages.

Many of the nation's largest corporations have begun to videotape their annual reports for stockholders, financial analysts, employees, local civic organizations, and even the general public through cable television. If a national trade association has the capability to videotape its own annual report, why not extend that to providing the same service, at a fee, to its members?

For example, assume an association for life insurance companies has a staff of trained experts who know and understand the industry. It also hires a writer/producer trained in the production end of videotaping, including camera techniques and editing. The association contracts with a free-lance photographic firm and produces an annual report for the industry.

With the association's life insurance knowledge, the writer/producer is made available to member companies for videotaping their annual reports, on a cost-plus-fee basis. Members would have the backing of a writer and staff who truly understand the life insurance industry, rather than the usual commercial film production companies.

Nonprofit films and videocassettes can be entertaining as well as informative. Just as there are books on every subject, videos can be produced to match the interest, sports, or hobbies represented by individual member organizations. Now that the VCR is available in the majority of U.S. households, members can be sold videos as well as books, through promotion in nonprofit organization newsletters and magazines.

Production costs for entertainment videos can be expected to exceed that of business videos, but the potential market is much greater. Associations for skiers and drag racing can produce videotapes and sell them to skiing and drag-racing enthusiasts as well as to their members; the same is true of other sports and hobbies. Even stamp collectors might enjoy seeing the latest issues in full color.

Filming or videotaping opportunities are not limited to national associations. Local organizations can also produce and sell videos to other, similar organizations and their members. Just as local educational television stations have produced some of public television's finest programs, the same can be true of local nonprofit groups.

Skiing associations in Colorado, Utah, or Vermont could provide videos of interest to all skiers. Birdwatchers in any location could document the feathered fliers in their area. The same is true of sailing, horse-breeding, or fishing enthusiasts.

In providing information and entertainment services, newsletters and magazines are the wheat; special reports, books, and audiovisual materials are the bread; but computer services are today's cake.

Computer Services

Since the advent of desk computers, nonprofit organizations are developing and subscribing to databases, then making them available to members. The computerized information may be retained in-house, and tapped into by members, or sold to members and nonmembers on *diskettes*.

The U.S.-China Business Council packaged a *Special Report on U.S. Investment in China* with a *Computerized Investment Datafile* diskette, and sold it for $185 to member companies and $250 to nonmembers.

The *Investment Datafile* has 517 U.S. investment projects in China, each with more than 30 database fields: investment partners, addresses, contract types and equity, locations, industrial sector, and other key information.

Members can use their own software to sort and cross-reference database fields to create specialized reports or letters. With the address for each project, they can generate mailing labels and send tailored letters to investment projects in a particular region, industry, or other market segment.

The accompanying *Special Report* assesses recent changes in China's investment climate and how investors are responding to new challenges. Case studies examine the successes and mistakes of other investors in China.

The U.S.-China Business Council's investment package is invaluable to members doing business in China, and to potential members investigating investment opportunities. This would be an enormous expense for a single company to undertake, yet it provides a needed service that is revenue-producing for the council.

The National Association of Chain Drug Stores takes a different approach to its computer services. NACDS has an in-house database which indexes periodical articles and publications related to its industry, and subscribes to external on-line databases which allow for a broader search of industry information.

Full-text articles in newspapers and magazines, bibliographic references to pharmaceutical publications, and business information pertaining to companies can be searched on-line for a nominal fee based on time spent and the database searched.

NACDS also offers its members a *Computer Bulletin Board System* for direct on-line communications with other members and with the association. Through the *Bulletin Board*, members can send and receive electronic messages, share documents and business reports, distribute and receive files, and access updated summaries from NACDS on important legislative and regulatory matters.

This is the electronic service as described by NACDS to its members:

1. Access the Bulletin Board by telephoning it via your computer modem . . .
2. Read the updated bulletins on NACDS events and important industry news items.
3. Join "conferences" (a group of messages devoted to a single topic of interest—such as NACDS Advisory Committees, state legislative and regulatory issues, federal issues and events, etc.).
4. Leave messages, comments, or items of interest for other members or for NACDS staff to read.
5. Copy (or download) files for your own use. Current files include NACDS information, state issues, federal issues, FDA information, spreadsheet templates, graphic charts, and more. These files include analyses of pharmaceutical manufacturing pricing trends (from Medi-Span's MDDB-Select database), state and federal legislative and regulatory initiatives, and tools to help you analyze your business.
6. Copy files to the Bulletin Board for other members to use.

The electronic bulletin board is the ultimate service for hands-on computer users. It is a two-way "wire service"—members are kept informed daily, and they also have the capability to interact with their association and other members in the same business or profession.

Although many nonprofits are currently investigating the possibilities of electronic mail and computer services, possibilities exist for nearly every budget. Information and messages could be exchanged without industry databases developed in-house, for example.

The National Association of Broadcasters has sophisticated in-house computer capability, but does not communicate directly with members computer-to-computer. Instead, its Library and Information Service subscribes to several research services that provide information from more than 800 databases:

DIALOG—includes databases such as *Harvard Business Review, Books in Print,* and *UPI News,* as well as indices such as *Trade and Industry Index* (trade publications), *Legal Resource Index,* and *Magazine Index* (which covers 435 popular magazines).

VUTEXT and DATATIMES—news-oriented with emphases on U.S. newspaper coverage.

WILSONLINE—includes indices such as *Business Periodicals Index, Readers' Guide to Periodical Literature,* and *Index to Legal Periodicals.*

NEWSNET—database search for newsletter coverage.

Most of the information retrieved through NAB's Online Database search service is bibliographic. It usually includes title, author, publication date, and a summary of the article. Occasionally, the full text of a magazine or newspaper article is available. According to NAB, on-line search costs range from a few dollars to a few hundred dollars, depending on which database is searched and the length of the search.

Computerized services to members are expected to grow at a faster rate than most other sources of nondues revenue. Today's workforce, nurtured on television and Nintendo®, are as comfortable with computers as their parents were with radios and typewriters. Innovations will trickle up to management, and management should listen to its computer techies.

Consulting Services

Companies entering new areas of business often turn to outside consultants to avoid costly mistakes. They may need proprietary marketing research or intensive briefings by experts, but they are looking for the best.

This is an area capably fulfilled by many nonprofit trade organizations. The U.S.-China Business Council is an excellent example. It provides tailored consulting services for its new members—U.S. companies interested in doing business in China.

With offices and resources in Washington and Beijing, the council conducts market surveys in China, using dependable Chinese field researchers. Staff analysts design, implement, and analyze the surveys, then prepare report presentations. This is an exclusive service for members, done on a fee basis.

For companies seeking investment opportunities, the council offers half- to one-day briefings. Every aspect of investing in China is explored. Depending on the companies' goals, the council helps members plan the best investment form, whether an equity joint venture, contractual joint venture, or wholly owned subsidiary.

The U.S.-China Business Council also helps a company member with a strategy session when there is a need to anticipate or understand Chinese regulations and economic policies, or an unforeseen issue or regulatory change occurs.

Expatriate orientations are another valued service available to member employees who are moving to China. They are briefed on China's history, culture, politics, and economy. Chinese life is described in detail, as well as attitudes, daily lives, family and social relationships, customs, and courtesies of the Chinese people. Trip preparation, including medical and financial considerations, shipping, living conditions and work environment are discussed thoroughly in one- to two-day sessions.

Trade associations are unique in their ability to provide a variety of consulting services to their members. They have economists, engineers, and attorneys who understand the problems peculiar to the industry they serve. Management, technical, and legal information provided by the staff to all members can be tailored to the particular needs of individual company members.

Associations that conduct industrywide research can just as easily provide proprietary research for individual members. Specific questions may be piggybacked onto a national study, or a separate study may be conducted for a single member. Oversampling in a region may assist members with regional sales problems. Why shouldn't they take advantage of their association's research capabilities? Who would have a better understanding of their business?

Employee training is another consulting service that can be made available to individual members. Since many organizations produce both written and audiovisual training materials, they could expand this by offering specialized training classes at the association headquarters or company locations.

All of the information services described above focus on member needs. Publications, audiovisual materials, computer, and consulting services are important sources of nondues revenue to nonprofit organizations, but essentially they are an extension of benefits tailored to the varied interests, concerns, and requirements of their members.

The next source of revenue to be examined, advertising, is not essential to nonprofits' member needs. The revenue produced from advertising, however, can make significant contributions to the non-revenue-producing arms of the operation such as government relations, or to General and Administrative (G&A) expense overhead.

7. Advertising

Most nonprofits use newsletters as their primary means of communicating with members. The newsletter is a timely device for informing members of occurrences within their industry, profession, or common interest; problems with the current administration, Congress, and state and local governments; and the latest developments within the organization.

Smaller nonprofits accomplish this informative task with a monthly newsletter; larger groups have biweekly or weekly newsletters, depending on their affluence or the urgency of impending issues.

Many national trade associations and individual member organizations also publish a monthly or bimonthly magazine with readership extending beyond their members. Although a few timely items may be inserted just before going to press, a magazine's real strength is treating members' interests with more extensive coverage through articles, reports, and analyses. Since a magazine usually has coated paper stock that reproduces color photographs and charts very well, it is often a prestigious hallmark of the industry or profession the association represents.

When to Accept Advertising

When should a nonprofit organization publication accept advertising? Only when advertising is expected to produce a sufficient increase in net revenue to justify the expense, effort, and supervision required.

Before deciding to accept advertising, the publication editor and publisher should consider these vital questions:

1. Who are our readers?
2. How many readers are there?
3. What is the publication's frequency?
4. What are the printing and distribution costs?
5. How much could be charged for advertising?
6. What is the estimated gross advertising revenue?
7. What would be the cost of sales?
8. What is the minimum estimated net revenue?
9. Is it worth it?

1. Who are our readers? Think in terms of potential advertisers. What do the readers buy, and what purchases do they influence?

In business or their professions, are the member-readers buying or approving the purchase of industrial products or equipment; office and telecommunications equipment; accounting, insurance, financial, legal, transportation, or consulting services?

Are they frequent business travelers? Do they fly frequently, rent cars, stay in moderate to expensive hotels, arrange meetings?

Outside their place of business, what are the readers' life-styles? Can they afford to buy new luxury cars; take summer and winter vacations; purchase expensive jewelry, wines, and liquors? Most luxury goods advertisers cannot afford television; would they be willing to pay a high cost per thousand to target readers in a position to buy?

The editor should have a general grasp of the buying power and personal life-styles of a publication's readers before documentation through marketing research. That comes later, after considering circulation, frequency, and cost, when the decision has been made that accepting advertising is feasible.

2. How many readers are there? Circulation is important to advertisers. If a newsletter has only a few hundred readers, or a magazine only a few thousand, it may attract those businesses specializing in that particular industry or profession, but it will be difficult to entice broad business and consumer advertisers other than those with directly related products.

For example, a newsletter with a small circulation might carry service and equipment advertising applicable only to the readers' business or profession, but not products or services that could be sold to all businesses such as office, computer, and telecommunications equipment advertising found in *Business Week, Forbes,* or *Fortune.*

If, however, the publication is a respected magazine with circulation of 25,000 or more, there could be sales potential for national business and industrial advertisers. With a circulation of 50,000 to 100,000 a magazine might even appeal to potential consumer advertisers.

Consider an airline. If its air routes extend from the United States to the Far East, and a publication's readers travel frequently to the Far East, it might advertise despite the limited number of readers. A regional airline might be attracted to an association publication whose member-readers are heavily concentrated in the region it serves.

A major carrier throughout the United States would hardly be interested in a magazine with a circulation of less than 50,000 until it was convinced the readers were frequent fliers for both business and pleasure. A magazine with more than 100,000 circulation would receive serious evaluation by nearly all the airlines with national advertising print budgets.

3. *What is the publication's frequency?* Potential advertisers are concerned with the purchasing capabilities of a publication's readers and the number who read it, but frequency assists the association in determining the projected advertising revenue. Is it published every week, twice a month, monthly, or every other month? Frequency makes a tremendous difference in total revenue.

A monthly newsletter with 500 readers (other than Fortune 500 CEOs) has limited potential for producing additional association revenue. The small circulation limits the number of advertisers, and publication only 12 times per year limits the total gross revenue.

If a newsletter has a circulation of 5,000 to 10,000 and is published every week or twice a month, the advertising dollars per issue may be slightly less than a monthly, but total advertising revenue should be nearly doubled or quadrupled.

Increased frequency shortens the reader life of a newsletter or magazine. The advertiser who runs six times in a monthly often schedules 12 insertions in a semimonthly or 26 in a weekly, to ensure being seen in every other issue.

Many nonprofit organizations publish a magazine every other

month. Does such a low frequency diminish its advertising potential? Not necessarily. Again, consider the nature and number of the readers and their purchasing habits. A bimonthly with a circulation of fewer than 10,000 might be marginal until its readers' buying power is documented through market research. Consumer advertising would be limited.

Using the airlines again as an example, air freight or overseas business travel might be advertised, but not family pleasure travel. The cost per thousand would be prohibitive.

Few nonprofit magazines are published more frequently than monthly, making circulation the deciding factor. With 25,000 to 50,000 readers a magazine has the potential to generate a substantial number of advertising pages per issue from business and industrial advertisers, particularly those specializing in manufacturing products or delivering services to the industry or profession represented by the association.

Not all nonprofit organizations are trade associations; a large number are societies with thousands of individual members, including professional associations of accountants, attorneys, doctors, and real estate brokers, or societies with families as members according to their interests, such as the National Geographic Society and the Smithsonian Institution.

Magazine circulation of these individual member organizations can easily exceed 100,000, with a few higher than one million. They are extremely attractive to major consumer advertisers selling travel, insurance, computers, books and videos, and financial services, as well as to advertisers of products or services peculiar to the readers' interests.

Magazines with circulations of more than 100,000 can be expected to contribute substantial net revenue to their associations or societies, providing expenses are closely controlled.

4. *What are the printing and distribution costs?* Before advertising rates are set, examine the publication's printing and distribution costs. Editorial and circulation expenses are not a factor with an established publication, as they are already built into the organization's budget.

Determine the existing publication's average printing and distribution cost per issue for the past 12 months, then add 10 percent to cover unexpected cost increases in the year ahead. Divide the cost per issue by the average number of pages printed per issue to derive the estimated printing and distribution cost per page for the coming year (see figure 3-3).

5. How much could be charged for advertising? With an estimated cost per page for printing and distribution, the association has a basis for determining its advertising rates. In figure 3-3 the monthly magazine with 100,000 circulation expects to spend $642 per page, whether or not it accepts advertising. That is a cost per thousand (CPM) of $6.42, well below current ad rates.

It is desirable to set a publication's advertising page rate at approximately three times its printing and distribution cost. In this case the rate would be just over $1,900 per black-and-white page, at a CPM of

Figure 3-3. Estimating Printing and Distribution Costs for a Monthly Magazine with Circulation of 100,000

Past 12 Months Actual Costs:	12 Months Total	Cost Per Issue
Printing	$225,588	$18,799
Paper	291,864	24,322
Postage & Dist.	154,992	12,916
Total	$672,444	$56,037
Number of Pages Printed	1,104	92
Average Cost per Page	$609	$609
Estimated Costs for Next 12 Months Actual Printing, Paper & Postage Costs	$672,444	$56,037
10% Estimated Cost Increase for Next 12 Months	67,244	5,604
	$739,688	$61,641
Estimated Number of Pages to Be Printed	1,152	96
EST. COST PER PAGE	$642	$642

$19. Smaller advertisements would be priced proportionately higher, and there would be a substantial premium for color.

Does this match competitive publication rates? Competitors of the monthly magazine depicted in figure 3-3 have black-and-white page rates that vary from $18 to $41 per thousand, making $19 a reasonable CPM.

Generally, small-circulation publications with higher page costs also have targeted audiences that justify a high CPM. As circulations rise, CPMs usually drop.

Figures 3-4 and 3-5 examine selected publications owned by non-profit organizations, comparing the relationship of their advertising page rates and CPMs to their total circulation.

Business-oriented publications listed in figure 3-4 have striking extremes in circulation, page rates, and CPMs. *The China Business Review*, published by the U.S.-China Business Council, has a circulation of little more than 3,000, but its readers are high-income executives who are frequent travelers to the Far East, with proven purchasing power within their multinational corporations. *The China Business Review* commands a CPM of more than $400.

Association Management, published by the American Society of Association Executives (ASAE), has approximately 21,000 circulation. It has tremendous appeal to hotel and travel advertisers since ASAE members are in a position to choose convention sites, hotels, and airlines. *Association Management* has a CPM of nearly $150.

Computer, published by the IEEE Computer Society, has close to 100,000 circulation, and although its readers are influential users and buyers of computers and software, its CPM is just over $40, probably due in part to the intense competition among computer magazines.

To be expected, the two publications with the largest business-oriented circulations have the lowest CPMs. *Nation's Business*, owned by the U.S. Chamber of Commerce, and *Real Estate Today*, published by the National Association of Realtors, have circulations of 800,000 or more, with CPMs of $26 and $21, respectively.

Note that even the smallest circulation magazine, *The China Business Review*, charges $1,400 per advertising page, more than the $1,000 considered to be the minimum. *Nation's Business*, with its high circulation and low CPM, receives $22,350 per advertising page.

Selected consumer-oriented publications owned by nonprofit

Figure 3-4. Business-Oriented Publications Owned by Nonprofit Organizations

Title	Publisher	Issues Per Year	Circulation	Advertising Page Rate	Cost Per M
The China Business Review	U.S.–China Business Council	6	3,327	$ 1,400	$424.24
Credit Union Management	Credit Union Executive Society	12	5,425	1,350	250.00
Iron & Steel Engineers	Association for Iron & Steel Engineers	12	10,708	1,750	163.55
Association Management	American Society of Association Executives	12	20,877	3,050	145.93
Savings Institutions	U.S. League of Savings Institutions	12	21,770	3,165	145.18
Automotive Exec.	National Automobile Dealers Assn.	12	22,338	3,110	139.46
Food Technology	Institute of Food Technologists	12	26,501	2,500	94.34
Constructor	Association General Contractors of America	12	29,195	2,445	83.73
Fire Journal	National Fire Protection Association	6	53,007	3,500	66.04
Management Accounting	National Association of Accountants	12	87,604	4,335	49.49
Computer	IEEE Computer Society	12	94,033	4,080	43.40
Chemical and Engineering News	American Chemical Society	52	129,746	7,680	59.21
ABA Journal	American Bar Association	12	400,646	11,475	28.64
Real Estate Today	National Association of Realtors	10	796,641	17,000	21.33
Nation's Business	Chamber of Commerce of the United States	12	858,228	22,350	26.05

Source: SRDS Business Publication Rates & Data, October 24, 1990.

organizations are compared in figure 3-7. Most readers belong to associations or societies with special individual or family interests including health, conservation, travel, and horse breeding, among others.

Consumer advertisers, unlike many business advertisers, carefully scrutinize CPMs when selecting print media. The smallest publication listed, *Skeet Shooting Review*, published by the National Skeet Shooting Association, has a circulation of 14,000 with the highest CPM, just under $70. The Marine Corps Association's *Leatherneck* magazine has approximately 100,000 circulation with a CPM of $18.

Half the magazines listed have circulations exceeding one million; although their CPMs are all less than $15, they vary according to readers' purchasing power.

The American Automobile Association's *AAA World*, with close to 2.5 million subscribers, commands only $9.13 per thousand, while *National Geographic*, with its higher-income and better-educated 10 million families, is in a position to charge a CPM of $13.43.

Modern Maturity, published by the American Association of Retired Persons, has a circulation of nearly 22.5 million. Understandably, *Modern Maturity* has the highest rate, $185,000 per advertising page, compared with *National Geographic*'s nearly $137,000 per page. Other than the two veterans' magazines owned by the V.F.W. and American Legion, *Modern Maturity* has the lowest CPM.

Notice once again that even the smallest circulation publication with the highest CPM, *Skeet Shooting Review*, has an advertising page rate close to $1,000.

Frequency, or the number of issues published annually, does not contribute to pricing the product, though it becomes extremely important when determining costs and projecting advertising revenue.

6. *What is the estimated gross advertising revenue?* To estimate revenue, begin with the number of advertising pages appearing in competitive publications. Normally it requires two or three years of concentrated effort to be added to an advertiser's schedule, and five or more years to replace an established competitor.

A small-circulation eight-page newsletter cannot expect to average more than three to five pages of paid advertising during its first two years of publication. Although its "house" advertising of services offered by the association will bring in revenue, that can be accom-

Figure 3-5. Consumer-Oriented Publications Owned by Nonprofit Organizations

Title	Publisher	Issues Per Year	Circulation	Advertising Page Rate	Cost Per M
Skeet Shooting Review	National Skeet Shooting Association	12	14,354	$ 992	$69.37
American Fitness	Aerobics & Fitness Assn. of America	6	25,200	1,180	46.83
The Quarter Horse Journal	The American Quarter Horse Association	12	68,209	1,120	16.42
Family Motor Coaching	Family Motor Coach Association	12	86,600	2,700	31.18
Leatherneck	Marine Corps Association	12	103,778	1,855	17.87
Sierra	Sierra Club	6	441,990	10,010	22.65
The Rotarian	Rotary International	12	529,020	6,220	11.76
American Rifleman	National Rifle Association of America	12	1,442,317	14,000	9.71
V.F.W. Magazine	Veterans of Foreign Wars of the U.S.	11	1,861,182	13,800	7.42
NEA Today	National Education Association	8	1,919,340	28,475	14.84
Smithsonian	Smithsonian Institution	12	2,295,985	33,715	14.68
AAA World	American Automobile Association	6	2,479,214	22,638	9.13
The American Legion Magazine	The American Legion	12	2,828,238	20,945	7.41
National Geographic	National Geographic Society	12	10,182,911	136,725	13.43
Modern Maturity	American Association of Retired Persons	6	22,443,464	185,010	8.24

Source: SRDS Consumer Magazine and Agri-Media Rates & Data, October 27, 1990

plished without accepting commercial advertising, and should not be included in the estimated gross income.

Association and other nonprofit magazines can be expected to carry an average of five to ten pages of advertising per issue the first two or three years they accept advertising. This depends on the quality of readers, their buying influences, and the number of potential advertisers appearing in similar or competitive publications. After a few years of intensive sales effort, magazines should carry 15 to 20 advertising pages each month, and even more in convention and special issues.

Convert the estimated number of pages into dollars, multiplying total pages by 120 percent of the black-and-white full-page rate. The 20 percent accounts for small-space advertisers who are actually paying more per page than full-page advertisers.

Estimating the small-circulation monthly newsletter at three pages per month would bring a total of 36 pages per year. With a $500 advertising page rate, multiply 36 times $600 ($500 × 120% = $600) for an estimated annual gross advertising revenue of $21,600.

A prestigious small circulation bimonthly magazine might be estimated to run eight pages per issue, or 48 advertising pages per year. With a $1,400 page rate, multiply 48 times $1,680 ($1,400 × 120% = $1,680), with an estimated annual gross revenue of $80,640.

The 100,000-circulation monthly magazine with the same estimated eight pages per issue and a $1,926 page rate would have 96 advertising pages, or $2,311 per page ($1,926 × 120% = $2,311), with estimated annual gross income of $221,856.

The newsletter appears to be marginal, the magazines interesting. But this is gross revenue and does not include the cost of sales.

7. *What would be the cost of sales?* Major expense items to be considered are agency discounts, advertising personnel, promotional materials and mailings, telephone, and general overhead (see figure 3-6).

Large advertisers use advertising agencies to prepare their materials and place advertising in selected media, while many smaller businesses place their ads directly with the publisher, often relying on the publication to set the type.

Recognized advertising agencies traditionally deduct 15 percent from published ad rates as their commission for preparing and placing

Figure 3-6. Estimating Publications' Net Revenue

	Monthly Newsletter	Bimonthly Magazine	Monthly Magazine
Circulation	1,000	4,000	100,000
Advertising Page Rate	$ 500	$ 1,400	$ 1,926
Cost per M	$ 500	$ 350	$ 19.26
Estimated Advertising Pages	36	48	96
Estimated Annual Gross Revenue	$21,600	$80,640	$221,856
ESTIMATED COST OF SALES			
Advertising agency discount		$ 6,048	$24,959
Salaried employee & benefits	$10,000	25,000	
Outside sales representative			43,317
Promotion & research materials	1,800	6,000	12,500
Telephone sales expense	900	1,440	
Promotional mailings postage	650	1,300	
General overhead (est. at 35% of gross revenue)	7,560	28,224	
Total Estimated Cost of Sales	$20,910	$68,012	$80,776
ESTIMATED NET REVENUE	$690	$12,628	$141,080
COST OF SALES % OF GROSS REVENUE	96.8%	84.3%	36.4%

the ads. The advertiser pays the full rate to the agency, and the agency deducts the 15 percent commission when invoiced by the publisher.

Few advertisers in small-circulation newsletters have agencies, but even then the newsletter can state on its advertising rate card, "Rates are noncommissionable," placing full payment responsibility on the advertiser.

Using the small-circulation bimonthly magazine as an example, it is estimated that 50 percent of the advertising might come through agencies, and the remaining half from advertisers without agencies. With gross revenue of $80,640, 15 percent commission on $40,320 totals $6,048.

The monthly magazine with 100,000 circulation is estimated to receive 75 percent of its revenue through advertising agencies, discounting 15 percent of three-quarters of its gross revenue for a total of $24,959.

Who would be responsible for advertising sales and advertising materials before they go to the printer? The small newsletter could probably manage with half of one staff person's time, estimated at $10,000, while the bimonthly magazine might require one full-time person, estimated at $25,000. It is doubtful that an experienced advertising representative would take it on a straight commission basis, since the gross would barely justify the representative's time and expenses.

The monthly magazine, however, could go either way by having an in-house advertising sales manager or an outside sales representative. In figure 3-6, expenses are based on the latter, assuming the representative would receive 22 percent commission on gross revenue, after agency discounts, or $43,317.

Other major expenses are promotion and research materials, promotional mailings, and telephone sales expense. With or without an advertising representative, an association should be responsible for the collection and printing of research and promotional materials, to be certain they properly reflect the organization and its publication. Promotional mailings, telephone sales expense, and travel and entertainment expenses, where required, are usually the responsibility of the outside sales representative as part of the agreement.

For general overhead expenses—including office space, furniture and equipment, office supplies, etc.—an arbitrary figure of 35 percent of gross revenue was used. Each association or society would take a much closer look, depending on its detailed expenses per employee. The small newsletter overhead is estimated at $7,560 and the bimonthly magazine at $28,224, which might be excessive. Since the monthly magazine has an outside sales representative, there would be no additional overhead expense.

Based on expenses outlined in figure 3-6, the newsletter cost of sales as a percentage of gross revenue is 97 percent; the bimonthly, 84 percent; and the monthly magazine, 36 percent. The advantages and disadvantages of advertising acceptance begin to emerge.

8. *What is the minimum estimated net revenue?* Gross revenue was based on the minimum number of advertising pages expected in the first two years. With an aggressive sales and marketing plan and proper

execution, each publication could increase its net revenue by one-to two-thirds within five years.

In terms of real dollars, tripling the net of $690 would do little for the newsletter. The bimonthly might throw off a positive cash flow of $25,000 if it doubled its net income in five years, while the monthly magazine could make a significant contribution to the association with only modest growth.

9. *Is it worth it?* Advertising cannot be claimed as a membership benefit, even though it is informative. If accepted, advertising's true purpose is to produce revenue. The excess of income over expenses is available to strengthen nonincome-producing departments such as government relations, or to improve the publication itself through the hiring of additional editorial staff, adding news pages, or increasing the use of color in its articles.

If the association with the monthly newsletter believed it vital to increase the frequency to 24 times per year, based on its members' information needs, it might possibly consider advertising acceptance. Its dollar potential would double with minimal increased costs of sales, though printing and distribution costs would also nearly double. As a monthly, however, it would be less bothersome without advertising.

The bimonthly magazine can generate sizable new income without increasing its frequency. It merely requires competent marketing research, planning, and consistent direct mail to potential advertisers with telephone follow-ups. Moving from six to 12 issues would result in a significant increase in editorial and printing expenses if it were to continue producing major articles and analyses. Unless its paid circulation climbed to nearly 20,000, with printing and distribution costs per page sharply lowered and advertising rate increased, it makes fiscal sense to continue publishing every other month.

The monthly magazine with 100,000 circulation is poised to take off. It would benefit little from more circulation, and certainly has the frequency. Among trade and professional magazines, after reaching the milestone of 100,000 circulation, the only real benefits of additional readers are the perception of growth and the ability to increase the advertising page rate without boosting the cost per thousand. This magazine simply requires research, planning, consistent direct mail and telephone follow-ups, and possibly personal contact with potential advertisers in metropolitan areas where they are concentrated.

As demonstrated, advertising is not always worth the expense and effort. Many associations have both a newsletter and a magazine where only the magazine accepts advertising. Usually this is a sensible approach, unless the newsletter is a semimonthly or weekly, and the organization has a strong sales staff with backup. Then sales can go beyond advertising to include other nondues revenue-producing activities such as exhibits, hospitality suites, promotional items, and publications.

Advertising Sales Materials

Whether advertising is sold by staff members inside the association or by outside representatives, the development of sales and research materials requires close supervision by the editor and executive director, who understand the publication, its member-readers, and the association's goals. Effective materials present an accurate portrayal of the publication and the association, consistent in appearance with other materials throughout the organization.

Advertising is a specialized field with specific rituals and requirements. An association that has a magazine with real advertising potential should seriously consider hiring an experienced advertising salesperson to develop the materials and sell the advertising before choosing outside sales representation. Even then, it would be helpful to have an advertising sales manager to work with, as well as supervise, the representatives.

What is required to sell advertising? Here are the basics prior to actual sales efforts:

1. List the publication in SRDS.
2. Print an advertising rate card.
3. Study the readers and their buying habits.
4. Prepare a media kit.
5. Compile lists of potential advertisers.

The SRDS Listing. Most inquiries for a copy of the magazine and media kit originate with SRDS, the Standard Rate and Data Service. Advertisers and advertising agencies depend on this monthly directory to plan their advertising campaigns. Unless a publication is listed in this directory, it will receive very few unsolicited inquiries from serious advertisers or their agencies.

SRDS lists magazines and tabloids by consumer and business categories in two separate directories. Each listing is free to the publisher, and it contains the following standardized information, where applicable:

Publisher's editorial profile
Personnel
Representatives and/or branch offices
Agency commission and cash discount
General rate policy
Advertising rates
    Black/white rates
    Color rates
    Covers
    Inserts
    Bleed
Classified/mail order
Split run
Special issue rates and data
Mechanical requirements and ad page dimensions
Issue and closing dates
Special services
Circulation
    Territorial distribution
    Business analysis of circulation

To be listed, SRDS requires a six-month sworn circulation statement from the publisher, using a standardized SRDS form. On the Consumer Magazine Statement it lists the date of first issue, single-copy price, and the name of the association publishing the magazine. It also provides space for the past six months' averages of total circulation, nonpaid and paid, subscriptions and single copy sales, and number of association members who are subscribers.

The reverse side of the SRDS circulation form has Geographical

Analysis of Circulation for a single issue by nine U.S. census regions, Canada, and foreign.

The SRDS sworn circulation statement does not carry the authenticity of a formal audit, but it informs the potential advertiser in a consistent manner of each publication's number of copies paid for or controlled through membership and newsstand sales, and the geographical distribution.

Advertising Rate Card. Listing in SRDS also requires the information necessary for an advertising rate card, the sales piece most often requested by interested advertisers.

A rate card contains a brief editorial description and profile of the publication's readers and a detailed rate breakdown by page size, frequency, and two- and four-color advertising.

Mechanical requirements have little to do with the sale of advertising, but are necessary for the production people who prepare the ads for placement. They include the magazine's trim size, screen preferred, type of printing, method of binding, bleed specifications, standard unit sizes, and reproducible requirements.

Nearly all the information listed in SRDS is included on most advertising rate cards. Until a media kit is complete, the magazine can reply to interested inquiries with the latest issue of the publication, a copy of the SRDS sworn circulation statement, and the advertising rate card.

Reader Research. The publication staff cannot know too much concerning its readers. The editor benefits from reader research by learning the readers' news interests. If the magazine, tabloid, or newsletter has special departments, readers can be asked to evaluate them, assign them relative importance, and make comments and suggestions for improving the product.

Editors and advertisers are interested in learning what other publications are read regularly by the magazine's subscribers. Nonduplication of readership with a competitive magazine that is on an advertising schedule is a strong argument for being added.

Most potential advertisers request more extensive information. Consumer advertisers ask for demographics including age bracket, marital status, sex, and family income of the publication's subscribers. They also request the percentage of subscribers who own homes, cars and trucks, insurance, credit cards, and consumer items. Even more useful is a demonstration of buying power in the past 12 months: air travel; car rentals; hotel stays; and purchases of motor vehicles, electronic equipment, clothing, and jewelry.

Business advertisers look for purchasing influence by the business or professional member-readers outside their homes. Are they corporate top management who must approve major purchases or middle management who specify the items purchased? Or are they self-employed owners of small businesses or professions? Are they frequent business travelers: where do they go, how do they go, where do they stay?

Extensive as it appears, most of this information can be developed by the publication with a three- or four-page questionnaire. With checklists, the subscriber can typically fill out a questionnaire in less than ten minutes. The only open-ended questions elicit comments or suggestions about the publication's news content. Not only will these comments be helpful to the editor, but many of the more positive statements will be invaluable for use in promotion pieces to demonstrate reader loyalty and acceptance.

The questionnaire can be prepared by the association with assistance from many books on the subject, or through the American Society of Association Executives (located in Washington, D.C.), which has extensive information available to nonprofit organizations.

Many associations turn to small outside marketing research firms capable of preparing the questionnaire, writing the covering letter, gathering an nth selection of subscribers for the sample mailing, tabulating the responses, and evaluating the results. Most independent research firms are relatively inexpensive, considering the time required to develop this information.

It is not advisable, however, to contract with marketing research firms or consultants unless they can demonstrate other studies completed for publications for the purpose of advertising sales. Pure editorial research experience is insufficient; researchers must understand the requirements of major advertisers and their advertising agencies.

One of the most reputable print media research firms is the Simmons Market Research Bureau in New York City. Its Custom Media Studies Division is capable of processing each step and delivering a professional study with a high return rate through the use of incentives and follow-up mailings. Its service is somewhat expensive, but well worth the price for publications with real advertising dollar potential.

Simmons will compare the findings with product and demographic data from its most recent "Study of Media and Markets," enabling a publication to identify areas of strength in selling advertising. It also includes a summary of findings along with the results of all Simmons subscriber studies in its booklet, UPDATE, which is mailed at no charge to the publisher and to its impressive list of advertiser and agency clients.

If the research is being conducted inside the association, select at least 1,000 subscribers on an nth name basis to ensure nearly 300 respondents. A publication with 10,000 subscribers selects every tenth name for the mailout. Approximately 30 percent can be expected to return the questionnaires without a follow-up mailing, and 300 replies are necessary to project the information to the total readership with meaningful percentages when cross-tabulations are involved.

A mailout of 1,000 is based on the number of expected returns, not the magazine's circulation. It would be equally acceptable for a publication with 100,000 circulation to select every 100th subscriber for a total of 1,000 names. With 300 returns the results are still projectable to the total readership and can be cross-tabulated into subcategories such as car buyers, new vs. used, or domestic vs. imports.

For a high rate of return, the cover letter is crucial. Signed by the editor, publisher, or executive director, the letter explains the urgency of completing and returning the questionnaire within a specified time.

Nearly one-third of subscribers should reply if properly convinced that 1) they have been selected at random; 2) the information requested is necessary for editors to meet their readers' information requirements; 3) advertisers are also interested in knowing what they read and purchase; and 4) the individual replies will remain confidential.

The mailout consists of an outside no. 10 envelope, affixed with a commemorative stamp for best results. Inside, it contains the cover letter, a three- or four-page questionnaire marked CONFIDENTIAL, and a postage-paid, self-addressed no. 9 envelope (see figure 3-7).

Within six weeks after mailout, approximately 300 returns should

Figure 3-7. *Leatherneck* Magazine Subscriber Questionnaire

MARINE CORPS ASSOCIATION

May 10, 1991

Dear LEATHERNECK subscriber:

We would appreciate your help in keeping us updated on your interests.

Our editors need to know the news subjects of greatest importance to you, and the ability to have top-quality advertising depends in part on the advertiser knowing more about you, including your travel and buying habits.

Would you please take just a few minutes to check the answers to the enclosed questions? You do not need to sign your name; your individual reply will be kept con- fidential.

It is very important to us to hear from you as we have selected your name as just one out of 100 of our sub- scribers to survey. In order for us to make an accurate projection of the results, we need your reply.

When you have completed the questionnaire, just return it to us in the enclosed postage-paid reply envelope no later than June 28, 1991.

Sincerely,

A. Lukeman

Anthony Lukeman
LtGeneral, USMC (Ret)
Executive Director & Publisher

CONFIDENTIAL

<u>LEATHERNECK QUESTIONNAIRE</u>

1. Please check your current <u>military status</u>:
   a) ___ Active Duty   ___ Reserve   ___ Retired   ___ Former Marine ___ Other
   b) Military Grade _____

2. Present <u>marital status</u>:
   a) ___ Single   ___ Married   ___ Widowed or Divorced
   b) ___ Male   ___ Female

3. Please write in your present <u>age</u>: _____

4. Have you <u>re-located</u> in the past 12 months? ___ Yes ___ No
   a) Do you expect to change locations in the next 12 months?
                        ___ Yes   ___ No   ___ Don't Know

5. Please check each of the following military publications that you
   <u>read regularly</u> (three out of four issues):

   ___ Leatherneck   ___ Navy Times
   ___ Marine Corps Gazette   ___ Off Duty
   ___ Military Lifestyle   ___ Salute
   ___ Other _____

6. Approximately <u>how many others</u> read your copy of <u>Leatherneck</u> each month?
   (Please write in the estimated number)
          ___ Marines   ___ Family Members   ___ Others

7. Please check the degree of interest you have in the following
   <u>Leatherneck monthly features</u>:

	Always Read	Usually Read	Sometimes Read	Never Read
Books Reviewed	___	___	___	___
Crazy Caption	___	___	___	___
Every Clime and Place	___	___	___	___
Gyrene Gyngles	___	___	___	___
Leatherneck Laffs	___	___	___	___
Leatherneck Line	___	___	___	___
Mail Call	___	___	___	___
Sound Off	___	___	___	___
We--The Marines	___	___	___	___

8. Please check the following <u>subjects</u> that you would like to see more of
   in <u>Leatherneck</u>:
   ___ Armor   ___ Old Photos   ___ Travel
   ___ Artillery   ___ History   ___ New Equipment
   ___ Aviation   ___ Humor   ___ Overseas Duty
   ___ Infantry   ___ Physical Fitness   ___ Women Marines
   ___ Weapons   ___ Personalities   ___ Sports
   ___ Commissioning   ___ Educational   ___ Specialized
       Programs   Opportunities   Training
   ___ Other _____

9. Do you and/or members of your family use the Commissary? ___ Yes ___ No

10. Do you and/or members of your family use the Exchange? ___ Yes ___ No

11. How many weeks did you <u>travel</u> away from your home or Base during the past 12 months?
    ___ Less than one week
    ___ One to less than two weeks
    ___ Two to less than three weeks
    ___ Three to less than four weeks
    ___ Four weeks or more

12. Please check if you have done any of the following <u>in the past 12 months</u>:

    ___ Flown on a commercial airline
    ___ Taken a passenger train
    ___ Traveled by interstate bus
    ___ Rented a car, van or truck
    ___ Hired a moving van
    ___ Stayed in a commercial hotel or motel

13. Please check each of the following types of <u>credit cards</u> that you own:

    ___ Bank Cards (MasterCard, Visa, etc.)
    ___ Department Store Cards (Sears, J.C. Penney, etc.)
    ___ Oil Company Cards (Exxon, Texaco, etc.)
    ___ Telephone Cards (AT&T, MCI, etc.)
    ___ Travel Cards (American Express, Diner's Club, etc.)

14. What types of <u>insurance</u> coverage do you presently have?

    ___ Group Life
    ___ Whole Life
    ___ Homeowners
    ___ Motor Vehicle
    ___ Personal Property
    ___ CHAMPUS Supplemental

    a) Have you <u>purchased insurance or changed insurance companies</u> in the past 12 months? ___ Yes ___ No

15. Have you purchased a <u>hard cover book</u> in the past 12 months?
    ___ Yes ___ No

    a) <u>If yes</u>, do you belong to a book club? ___ Yes ___ No

16. Please check the types of <u>motor vehicles owned</u>, and whether they are Domestic or Imports:

	Domestic	Imports
Passenger Car	____	____
Pickup Truck or Van	____	____
Motorcycle	____	____
Other _____	____	____

17. Have you or other family members purchased a motor vehicle in the past 12 months? ___ Yes ___ No
    a) If yes, please check the type of motor vehicle, and whether it was bought New or Used:

	Bought In Past 12 Months			
	Domestic		Imports	
	New	Used	New	Used
Passenger Car	____	____	____	____
Pickup Truck or Van	____	____	____	____
Motorcycle	____	____	____	____
Other _____	____	____	____	____

18. Do you plan to buy a motor vehicle in the next 12 months? ___ Yes ___ No
    a) If yes, please check the type of motor vehicle, and whether it will be Domestic or an Import:

	Plan To Buy In Next 12 Months			
	Domestic		Imports	
	New	Used	New	Used
Passenger Car	____	____	____	____
Pickup Truck or Van	____	____	____	____
Motorcycle	____	____	____	____
Other _____	____	____	____	____

19. Please check each of the following that you own, purchased in the past 12 months, or plan to buy in the next 12 months:

	Own	Bought In Past 12 Months	Plan TO Buy In Next 12 Months
Electronics & Sound Equipment			
AM/FM Stereo Car Radio	____	____	____
Cassette Player	____	____	____
Compact Disc (CD) Player	____	____	____
Personal Computer	____	____	____
Stereo System	____	____	____
Telephone Answering Machine	____	____	____
Video Cassette Recorder (VCR)	____	____	____
Video Camera	____	____	____
Athletic Goods & Equipment			
Sports Equipment	____	____	____
Athletic or Running Shoes	____	____	____
Other Sports Apparel	____	____	____
Other			
Binoculars	____	____	____
Camera	____	____	____
Luggage	____	____	____
Marine Corps Memorabilia	____	____	____
Ring	____	____	____
Sunglasses	____	____	____
Watch	____	____	____

COMMENTS: _____
_____
_____
_____

PLEASE RETURN THIS QUESTIONNAIRE IN THE ENCLOSED POSTAGE-PAID ENVELOPE. THANK YOU.

be ready for tabulating. The final report should include a brief description of how the study was conducted, along with a copy of the questionnaire and covering letter. The following, taken from the Marine Corps Association's *Leatherneck* magazine readership and purchasing study, establishes the return rate:

Nth name mailing	1,000
Undeliverable returns	9
Total deliverable	991
Number of returns	354
RESPONSE RATE	35.7%

Advertising agency media buyers tend to ignore research with an insufficient number of returns and a response rate under 25 percent. A reader research study conducted by an independent research firm will have higher credibility, but an association publication's in-house study will also be accepted when the questions are unbiased, the study is properly conducted, and the results are reasonable.

The Media Kit. Armed with a sworn circulation statement, advertising rate card, and a readership and purchasing study, a magazine has the essential elements for a media kit.

To all but the research-oriented major advertisers and their agencies, however, the detailed research study may seem ponderous. A promotion piece or brochure that highlights the most favorable aspects of the study can broaden its appeal. An attractive brochure capably summarizes all of the publication's advertising values, including:

1. reader demographics
2. ownership and purchasing habits
3. favorable reader comments
4. comparative rates and CPMs
5. non-duplicated readership
6. circulation and advertising growth

Other than the magazine itself, the brochure will be the first piece in a media kit to catch a potential advertiser's eye.

The brochure has other valuable uses. It can be folded into eight panels, with one panel reserved for a reply card requesting the magazine and media kit. For mass mailings to large numbers of potential advertisers, the brochure with a strong cover letter will induce many to fill out and return the reply panel in the accompanying postage-paid, self-addressed reply envelope (see figure 3-8).

Other marketing and media information may be included in the media kit, depending upon the marketing information available for an industry or profession and the competitive position of the publication:

1. Annual purchases made by the association's total industry or profession
2. Editorial profile with a description of special Issues
3. Complete list of advertisers during the past 12 months (only when the list is impressive)
4. Advertising page rates and CPMs compared with competitive magazines

With this comprehensive media kit and a listing in SRDS, the association is prepared to sell advertising. But who will buy it?

Targeting Potential Advertisers. Identifying potential advertisers is a process to be initiated before the research study questionnaire is developed, and to be completed by the time sales materials are prepared.

Any number of companies may appear to be logical advertisers, but logic is not the key. Budgets are the determining factor. Which companies are budgeted to advertise in the publication's marketing coverage area? Do they currently advertise in business or consumer print media? Are they advertising in competitive magazines?

Take, for example, an association magazine in the field of state and local government. To target its potential advertisers, it would turn to the SRDS Business Publication Rates and Data Directory's section on government/public works. Each competitive publication would be recorded, with its circulation and advertising page rate, which is also useful for comparative purposes. Many of the competitive publications listed could be found in the association's library, since they all serve

Figure 3-8. *Leatherneck* Magazine Media Kit Brochure

LEATHERNECK

MAGAZINE OF THE MARINES

Marketing Highlights

In the past 12 months. . .

* 78% stayed in a hotel/motel

* 67% flew a commercial airline

* 41% rented a car

* 18% took a passenger train

* 23% bought a *new* passenger car

* 11% bought a *new* pickup truck or van

* 40% purchased insurance

* 37% bought athletic shoes

* 22% bought sports equipment

* 24% bought a wrist watch

* 18% bought an AM/FM stereo car radio

* 18% bought a VCR

* 15% bought a camera

* 9% bought a stereo system

* 6% bought a personal computer

LEATHERNECK - - A Marine Tradition. . .

Published each month for the past 72 years, *Leatherneck* magazine is a tradition with active duty Marines and Reserves, retired and former Marines -- officers and enlisted.

Leatherneck is a general purpose magazine designed to inform and entertain its 108,000 paid subscribers. Total readership is over 400,000, including an additional 123,000 Marines, 95,000 family members, and others.

Leatherneck informs and entertains by highlighting today's Marines, the duty they perform, where they serve, the importance of physical and mental fitness, and new weapons and equipment developments.

Leatherneck is the only magazine issued to every Marine undergoing recruit training. By the time training is completed, young Marines accept *Leatherneck* as a true reflection of life and pride in the Marine Corps. More than 80% of last year's recruits subscribed to *Leatherneck* after they completed training. Former Marines also like to keep up with the Corps by reading *Leatherneck.*

Reader loyalty to *Leatherneck* is intense. The Reader Comments will help you understand the fierce loyalty portrayed both to the Marine Corps and to *Leatherneck* -- Magazine of the Marines.

Subscriber Profile

AGE		
	Under 25	30%
	Under 35	40
	Under 45	65
SEX	Male	96%
	Female	4
MARITAL STATUS	Married	62%
	Single or Other	38
MILITARY STATUS	Active Duty & Reserves	*51%
	Former Marines	33
	Retired Marines	16
MILITARY RANK	Officers	17%
	Enlisted	83

*Based on 72,000 individual paid subscribers only. Active Duty proportion would be much higher if the study included readers of the 36,000 subscriptions purchased and distributed by the USMC throughout every Marine Base, recruiting stations, etc.

. . .Marines on the Move

TRAVEL AND TRANSPORTATION IN THE PAST 12 MONTHS

Transportation & Lodging		Weeks Traveled:	
Stayed in a hotel/motel	78%	1 Week or More	87%
Flew a commercial airline	67	2 Weeks or More	73
Rented a car or truck	41	3 Weeks or More	55
Took a passenger train	18	4 Weeks or More	39
Traveled by interstate bus	13		

. . .Active Owners and Buyers

Credit Cards Owned		Insurance Coverage	
Bank Cards	69%	Motor Vehicle	92%
Department Store	63	Homeowners	57
Telephone	48	Group Life	51
Oil Company	43	Whole Life	47
Travel Cards	21	Personal Property	46
		Champus Supplemental	13

OWNED AND BOUGHT IN THE PAST 12 MONTHS

Motor Vehicles	Own	Bought In Past 12 Months
Passenger Cars	87%	40%
Domestic Cars	68	29
Imported Cars	32	12
Pickup Trucks & Vans	47%	18%
Domestic	38	14
Imported	10	4
Motorcycles	11%	3%
Electronics and A/V Equipment		
AM/FM Stereo Car Radio	74%	18%
VCR (Video Cassette Recorder)	64	18
Cassette Player	70	16
Telephone	67	14
Stereo System	63	9
CD (Compact Disc) Player	18	9
Video Camera	13	4
Athletic Goods and Equipment		
Athletic or Running Shoes	73%	37%
Sports Apparel	51	23
Sports Equipment	60	22
Miscellaneous		
Marine Corps Memorabilia	70%	27%
Wrist Watch	74	24
Camera	71	15
Sunglasses	62	19
Ring	56	12
Luggage	58	10
Binoculars	49	5

SOURCE: 1989 *Leatherneck* Magazine Readership and Purchasing Study.

...Reader Loyalty And Participation

There is a 2-way communication between *Leatherneck* editors and their readers. These Marines are loyal to the Corps and to their magazine, *Leatherneck*. Beyond loyalty, however, they actively participate in communicating their ideas and news preferences to *Leatherneck* editors.

Reader Comments

- My first subscription to *Leatherneck* started when I attended Marine Corps Boot Camp in San Diego. I never intended to subscribe but I'm very glad I did. Cpl
- I like to read *Leatherneck*. It's an informative magazine about Marines. I would like to see more on Infantry. LCpl
- Photos keep the magazine alive. Photos of people rather than just inert equipment. LtCol
- I think the *Leatherneck* is a good magazine. I would like to see more training articles. I like to see everyone training hard and ready to accomplish the mission. Sgt
- Do not see anything that needs changing in *Leatherneck*. Has the right balance and coverage of events now. Cpl
- I think *Leatherneck* magazine is great! GySgt
- Hope you continue to look for new books, publications et al on Korean War. Capt
- Plan to attend OCS in a few years and would like to know how it is to become commissioned. PFC
- I have always purchased what is advertised in *Leatherneck*. If it's in *Leatherneck* I know it's the best quality for my money. Sgt
- You guys should put more time on the Reserve end of the stick. They're just as important ! ! ! Semper Fi. LCpl
- *Leatherneck* is an outstanding magazine. I would like to see a lot more on women Marines. Sgt (WM)
- Enjoyed *Leatherneck* on active duty and enjoy reading since retiring. It helps keep me informed about the Corps. Ret. MSgt
- Appreciate cartoons, complete coverage of events and Bases-Worldwide. CWO
- I feel proud to be a Marine every time I pick up a copy of *Leatherneck* magazine. Keep up the good work. Semper Fi. SSgt

LEATHERNECK

MAGAZINE OF THE MARINES

Tel. (703) 640-6161

Box 1775, Quantico, VA 22134

Please send the complete report on *Leatherneck* readership and purchasing information.

I would like to see a Media Kit with a recent issue of *Leatherneck*.

We may be interested in advertising. Please call me.

NAME _____

TITLE _____

COMPANY _____

ADDRESS _____

CITY _____

STATE, ZIP _____

TEL. NO. _____

state and local governments. If not, they may be available at the nearest public business library.

By going through back issues of each competitive publication, major categories and individual companies emerge. By Tearsheeting (ripping out) or copying the ads and sorting them by types of products and services, the advertising salesperson identifies companies and categories presenting the greatest potential. Although there are hundreds of companies that manufacture fire, water, and waste water; air pollution control; and data processing equipment for sale to state and local governments, fewer than 200 may be currently advertising in competitive magazines. They clearly have established budgets for state and local government advertising.

Companies committed to advertising in the same field of endeavor deserve the highest priority. In planning the purchasing portion of the subscriber study questionnaire, their marketing requirements are worth serious consideration.

Identifying the companies with advertising budgets is a fairly simple process, but targeting the decision makers within the companies and their advertising agencies requires persistence and tact.

Nonprofit organizations in pursuit of advertising income are prudent to invest in the two "Red Books," essential tools in advertising sales. The National Register Publishing Company in Winnetka, Illinois, publishes the *Standard Directory of Advertisers*, or the "Advertisers' Red Book," and the *Standard Directory of Advertising Agencies*, known as the "Agency Red Book."

The Advertisers' Red Book contains nearly 20,000 corporations by advertising categories. Most listings have the company's address; telephone number; products and services advertised; names and titles of the CEO and marketing and advertising directors; the advertising agency; and the latest annual advertising appropriations by types of media, including newspapers, consumer magazines, and business publications.

With the names of companies currently advertising in competitive magazines and the Red Books, the publication's advertising salesperson can identify the decision makers. A telephone call to each company will verify the name, title, and address of the manager in charge of the products being advertised.

When an advertising agency is involved, the company advertising manager is asked to identify the agency and account executive. By referring to the Agency Red Book, the account executive is called to identify others in the agency who are involved in the media selection process for the specific campaign appearing in competitive magazines. Key agency personnel to be added to the target list are the account executive, media director, and media planner or buyer.

After the company and agency telephone calls, the publication will have its "A" list of potential advertisers with the highest priority.

The "B" list, also taken from the Red Books, does not require telephone follow-up calls. A nonprofit with a consumer magazine simply takes each classification with major advertisers in competitive magazines, eliminates companies on the "A" list, and identifies the remaining companies that budget for advertising in consumer magazines. Organizations with business publications follow the same procedure, except they identify companies with budgets for advertising in business publications.

A list is compiled of the advertising managers with their addresses and telephone numbers from the Advertisers' Red Book. For companies listing advertising agencies, a referral to the Agency Red Book provides the names of account executives and media directors, who are also added to the "B" list.

If you are confused, return to the magazine in the field of state and local government. After tearsheeting advertisers in the competitive magazines taken from the SRDS listing of government/public works, it was discovered that most major advertisers fell into these Advertisers' Red Book classifications:

automobiles and trucks
electronics, radio, and television
industrial chemicals
insurance
lighting
machinery and supplies
office and data processing equipment
travel and transportation

The "A" list is made up of actual advertisers in the field, with follow-up calls that identify the key people in the company and agency, while the "B" list is derived from the remaining companies in the same classifications that budget for advertising in business publications.

An association with a consumer magazine directed to individual members might determine most advertisers in its field were under these Red Book classifications:

accessories, luggage, jewelry, etc.
apparel—men's and boys' wear
automobiles and trucks
banks, credit agencies, and investments
electronics, radio, and television
hotels, resorts, and real estate
insurance
office and data processing equipment
optical, photo, scientific instruments, and watches
sporting goods
travel and transportation
wines and liquors

This consumer magazine's "B" list is extracted from companies not known to be advertising in competitive publications, but listed in the above classifications as budgeting for advertising in consumer magazines.

Lists are valuable only when maintained. Tearsheeting the competition at least quarterly will add valuable potential advertisers to the "A" list. Checking names and addresses in the Red Books annually will update the "B" list.

When the "A" and "B" lists are in the computer or word processor and the media kit is fully assembled, the magazine has the essentials. There will be other lists for special issues, but at this stage the publication is strategically poised for serious advertising sales efforts.

Advertising Sales

If association management decides at the outset to enlist an outside sales representative, the person within the organization responsible for managing the representative should understand the necessary steps for successful selling.

Assume, however, that management decides to conduct its own sales activities for two years before considering an outside firm. One of the organization's more profit-oriented employees is appointed advertising sales manager, or an advertising professional is brought in as a full-time publication staff member.

The person responsible begins with a marketing plan, even though it may be revised through the learning process. The plan includes direct mail, telephone and follow-up correspondence, and personal meetings or sales calls with potential advertisers, when practical.

The marketing plan includes projected expenses for each sales activity. How many mailings will be sent? What are the projected printing and postage costs? How many telephone calls will be made? Should travel expenses be budgeted? Where to and how much?

When the marketing plan and estimated expenses are reviewed, revised, and approved by association management, the advertising sales manager has a budget. This protects the organization and frees the sales manager to proceed with the planned projects without the need for further approvals.

Direct Mail. Mailings are timed for maximum effect. Most large companies with extensive advertising budgets plan their various product campaigns months in advance. Advertising sales efforts are most productive when they coincide with advertiser and agency planning periods.

The majority of companies are on a calendar-year basis, with media planning underway between September and November for the following year. That definitely calls for a major September mailing.

Companies on a fiscal-year basis vary. January and February are excellent months for the publication to update its values and past year's accomplishments, such as advertising or circulation growth. A mailing in either month would coincide with fiscal year planning periods, which may start as early as March.

Two major mailings per year to lists of potential advertisers are the minimum. A publication with a convention issue where exhibitors are potential advertisers would send a third mailing to exhibitors. Other special issues would call for additional mailings to targeted prospects, rather than to the entire "A" and "B" lists.

The "A" list of companies and their agencies currently advertising in competitive magazines deserve the full treatment in September: a single-page cover letter, complete media kit with latest issue of the publication, mailed first class.

The cover letter is most effective when adapted to each advertiser's Red Book classification. Travel advertisers, for example, should receive a letter that leads off with the magazine's values as a travel medium, highlighting its readers' frequency of travel by air and destinations, and car and hotel rental information.

Other advertising values are included in the body of the letter, summarizing information available inside the media kit. It is advisable to limit the cover letter to a single page; advertising people have a notoriously short attention span.

The "B" list has a much broader audience of potential advertisers, known only to allocate budgets for consumer or business publications, according to the Red Book. Mailings to the "B" list weigh less, to hold down mailing costs.

The September mailing to the "B" list might be limited to a one-page cover letter, advertising rate card, brochure with built-in reply card (or separate reply card), and a no. 9-postage-paid, self-addressed envelope inside a no. 10 envelope, mailed first class.

If the "B" list is so large that cost is a factor, the mailing could be sent third class in zip code sequence, but that would prevent sending a cover letter tailored to specific advertising classifications.

In mass mailings, the cover letter's primary purpose is to generate requests for the media kit, with the names, addresses, and phone number of those interested on the return reply cards. Unless the potential advertiser writes, calls, or faxes for a media kit, that company remains on the "B" list. Advertisers who do respond are moved to the "A" list, where they can receive personal follow-ups.

January or February mailings to both lists can be limited to a single-page cover letter, brochure, rate card, reply device, and postage-paid reply envelope, mailed first class.

The winter mailing cover letter does not require customized treatment by advertising categories. It can lead off with any new developments during the past year, repeat the publication's advertising values, and again solicit a request for an updated media kit.

Convention issue, special issue, and directory mailings frequently appeal to smaller advertisers who do not have preplanned annual campaigns. Exhibitors may have a separate budget for advertising that will bring association members to their booths; others may advertise only in special issues whose theme is related to their products. Since there are major corporations with money set aside for special issues, the mailings are an opportunity to attract first-time advertisers who conceivably could be converted to full-schedule (six- or 12-page) advertisers in the years ahead.

Special issue cover letters should ask for the order. A flier describing the convention or special issue enables the advertiser to focus on the event; the brochure and advertising rate card describe the magazine's values; and a separate order card can urge a spontaneous decision.

The American Logistics Association (ALA) publishes a quarterly magazine, *Interservice*. The summer issue features the "ALA Brand Names & Suppliers Directory." Military managers of base commissaries and exchanges can look up a brand name such as Heinz and determine 1) the types of products available; 2) name and address of the manufacturer; 3) names of representatives or brokers in the military marketplace and; 4) how the base exchange or commissary can contact the nearest representative.

Companies selling the military market are anxious to promote their products to the readers of *Interservice*, particularly in the summer issue containing a directory that will be referred to for the next year. Figure 3–9 illustrates ALA's solicitation for advertisers for its "1991–92 Brand Names & Suppliers Directory."

The National Association of Broadcasters (NAB) has an interesting innovation—a directory of its associate members that lists their products and services, and is sent to "over **14,000** radio and television industry managers who are qualified to make buying decisions for the equipment, products and services they will use **throughout the entire year!**"

The NAB directory is a natural for obtaining substantial advertising revenue from associate members.

Advertising rates range from $50 to have the company name listed

Figure 3-9. American Logistics Association Solicitation for Special Issue Advertisers

 **AMERICAN LOGISTICS ASSOCIATION**

1133 Fifteenth Street, N.W. / Suite 640 / Washington, D.C. 20005 / (202) 466-2520
FAX: (202) 296-4419 / MCI Mail: 2459439 / Telex: 6502459439

March 15, 1991

TO: Commissary and Exchange Suppliers

FROM: Lisa Strauss, Advertising Manager

SUBJECT: ALA's "1991-92 Brand Names & Suppliers Directory"

INCREASE YOUR EXPOSURE IN THIS $14 BILLION MARKET THROUGH
ADVERTISING IN THE MOST COMPREHENSIVE BRAND NAMES DIRECTORY
AVAILABLE TO THE MILITARY RESALE INDUSTRY.

Now is the time to make your space reservations for the 1991
Summer issue of Interservice magazine. Featuring the "ALA Brand
Names & Suppliers Directory," this issue stands as a single
source of information on the military resale industry that
supplants any other reference document now available at the
commissary and exchange store level.

Highlights of this feature include: the kind of merchandise
represented by a particular brand name; who manufactures the
product; who represents them in the marketplace; and where and
how the exchange and commissary can contact them.

Take advantage of this opportunity to enhance your listing and
put your products in front of the personnel responsible for
making the buying decisions in the military marketplace each
and every time they refer to this valuable reference source.
Make your space reservations now for the 1991 Summer issue of
Interservice magazine. The ad close date for the Summer issue is
May 8 with a June 17 issue date.

The ad rates are as follows:

	Black & White	4-Color
Full page	$1,390	$2,375
2/3 page	960	1,945
1/2 page	840	1,825
1/3 page	775	1,760
1/4 page	710	1,700

If you would like to reserve space, or if you have any
questions, please give me a call at (202) 466-2520 or fax me at
202-296-4419.

ALA for the Promotion, Protection and Improvement of the Military Resale Industry in color to $1,200 for a full black-and-white bleed page to $4,500 for the back cover.

The first few paragraphs of the original announcement to NAB's associate members describe the new directory's benefits and sales possibilities:

THE NEW NAB BROADCAST RESOURCE GUIDE
TO PRODUCTS AND SERVICES

Spotlight On NAB's Associate Members . . .

Debuting in early 1990, the NAB *Broadcast Resources Guide* will feature:

- A complete listing of all NAB Associate Members, and *only* NAB Associate Members.
- Complete descriptions of the many broadcasting related products and services you provide, indexed for quick and easy reference.
- Contact information putting your products just a phone call away from broadcasters throughout the country.
- And best of all, listings in the Directory are *free* to all Associate Members!

After that glowing inducement to be listed in the directory, the brochure describes the advertising values to NAB's associate members:

The *Resource Guide* also presents an advertising opportunity for those who want to stand out in the crowd.

You can highlight your company name in color, lengthen your listing, or place an advertisement in the Directory that will give you increased visibility and showcase your products and services.

Considering the number of publications soliciting advertising today, advertising managers and agency media buyers have great difficulty distinguishing one from the other. Basic values cannot be repeated too frequently. If not followed through by telephone or in person, the average direct mail recipient might be two years away from being able to describe a publication and understand its advertising values.

Lists target potential advertisers; direct mail screens those with an immediate interest.

Telephone Follow-up. Two or three weeks after the media kit and magazine mailing to the "A" list, these potential advertisers should be telephoned.

Start with the advertising manager at the company who will either answer necessary questions or refer the caller to someone else in the company or at the advertising agency. Do not be discouraged by referrals; instead, keep a record of all those known to be involved in the media decision process and add them to the "A" list.

Advertising is seldom bought by a single person, though personal telephone contact may be limited to one person at the company and one or two at the agency. The entire decision team requires regular coverage by direct mail; telephone contacts can be as frequent as every 30 to 60 days, depending on the buying cycle.

On the initial telephone contact, attempt to ask these questions:

1. Do you remember seeing our media kit? (If not, briefly describe the publication.)
2. Do you have a budget for print advertising in our field?
3. In what publications are you currently advertising? When is your media planning period?
4. What can we do to be on your advertising schedule?
5. Should anyone else be contacted or added to our mailing list?

This information is extremely important. It should be recorded on computer or on a file card for each potential advertiser, to be used in subsequent calls or correspondence.

The first phone contact is not a sales call. Selling without proper information can set back the sale. Advertising professionals appreciate legitimate questions from a first-time caller; most will go out of their way to cooperate.

Backed with solid information, the caller has the ammunition to follow up with a sales letter that distinguishes the association's publication from its competitors', with detailed arguments for being included on the advertiser's schedule.

"B" list advertisers who respond with a request for a media kit require "A" list treatment. Shortly after the kit is mailed, the potential advertiser should be called. Information derived from that conversation forms the basis for a detailed follow-up sales letter.

The SRDS listing will also generate a steady stream of requests for media kits. These, too, should be added to the "A" list and pursued diligently, since they are potential advertisers with an immediate interest.

After each telephone call and follow-up correspondence to "A" list advertisers, copies of notes and letters should be assigned to a "call-back" file.

Without a callback file to refer to each week, the advertising salesperson may overlook the need to send an updated media kit, a periodic sales letter, or the next telephone inquiry to remain in the media decision process.

Selling advertising requires curiosity, patient persistence, and continuity. It is a very personal business, as is most long-term selling. For the publication to be accepted, the salesperson should be considered part of the team working together to increase the sales and profits of the advertiser.

Direct mail, telephone follow-ups, and individualized letters can be extremely effective over a period of two to three years. There is only one means of accelerating the process—personal, face-to-face contact.

Personal Contact. People like to know whom they are doing business with. When financially feasible, the publication's advertising sales manager or representative should meet periodically with major prospects and running advertisers. Personal contact hastens the sale and helps retain the valued advertiser.

For travel planning, sort the "A" list by zip code, then break down the companies and agencies by major metropolitan areas.

How many are within driving distance of the publication's headquarters? Meetings within 50 miles could be scheduled throughout the year, based on the advertisers' planning periods, without an overnight stay.

Prospective advertisers within 50 to 300 miles could be seen annually, by clustering scheduled appointments, with only one or two nights away from home.

Many publications find a heavy concentration of potential advertisers in New York, Chicago, and southern California. If the sales representative is located in or near one of these metropolitan areas, travel costs are greatly reduced.

What areas outside driving distance have the highest concentration of major prospective advertisers? Companies currently running six or more pages in competitive magazines require maximum priority.

Assume the magazine is located in the Washington, D.C., area and analysis reveals the top five metropolitan areas outside Washington with the largest number of prospects are Chicago, southern California, Dallas, New York, and Detroit.

Chicago has 54 companies and agencies on the "A" list, but only five advertisers running six or more pages in the field. In southern California, there are 50 prospects with 12 major advertisers; Dallas has 30 listed, but only two major advertisers; New York has 26 prospects including the agencies for 12 major advertisers plus four company headquarters; and Detroit, with only 15 advertisers and agencies, has eight companies or divisions running six-page plus schedules in the competition.

Here are the suggested priority rankings:

	Advertisers and Agencies:	
	Total	Major
1. Southern California	50	12
2. New York	26	16
3. Chicago	54	5
4. Detroit	15	8
5. Dallas	30	2

Southern California receives the highest ranking since it combines a large number of prospects with 12 major advertisers. Because of the driving distances and heavy freeway traffic, an advertising salesperson seldom manages more than three or four appointments a day. To be cost-effective, this trip requires a week's stay with 15 meetings scheduled in advance.

New York ranks second for two reasons. It has many of the nation's largest advertising agencies that specify the media schedules, and they are concentrated in Manhattan. With careful planning, an advertising sales person can achieve six appointments per day and have a profitable two-day trip with 12 meetings.

Chicago, with its large number of prospects, also requires annual attention, and can be covered in three days. The advertising agencies are grouped together around North Michigan Avenue, and most major corporate headquarters are located in the vicinity of O'Hare Airport. The salesperson should average four appointments per day, or 12 in three days.

Detroit is ranked ahead of Dallas because the automotive companies are heavy advertisers. If they are advertising in the magazine's competition, the car and truck advertisers and their agencies require personal attention, and even then it may be three to five years before they will add a new magazine to a schedule. It is possible to arrange four or five meetings per day in Detroit, but unless eight appointments can be scheduled in advance for a two-day stay, the trip should be postponed.

Dallas would be optional, although the number of prospects call for a two- or three-day stay at least every other year. The trip would be built around appointments with the two major advertisers, and the advertising salesperson can expect to average four meetings per day in the Dallas area.

Total travel costs should not exceed $125 per sales call, unless the traveler is addicted to the most expensive hotels. Five days in the Los Angeles-San Diego area with 15 appointments would allow $1,875 for airfare, car rental, food and lodging. Two days and nights in New York with 12 appointments should cost less than $1,500; three days in Chicago with 12 meetings, $1,500; two days in Detroit with eight sales calls, $1,000; and three days in Dallas with 12 meetings, $1,500. The Washington-based publication would spend far less than $1,500 on the New York trip because airfare would not be a major expense.

To others in the nonprofit organization it may seem unreasonable to spend between one and two thousand dollars for a sales trip, but assuming the advertising page rate exceeds $1,000, a trip that results in one or two pages of advertising will pay for itself. Most trips to cities other than Detroit will produce even more within one year, and persistence in Detroit could be richly rewarded in three to five years.

With an approved travel budget the advertising sales manager can schedule each trip well in advance. About three weeks ahead, letters are sent to every person on the "A" list within the metropolitan area, advising them of the date and purpose of the trip, and to expect a call the following week to arrange a definite appointment.

By including with the letter a copy of the latest issue, rate card, and descriptive brochure, the magazine to be discussed is identified, and even without the appointment, something has been accomplished. At least half the advertisers will be unable to see the salesperson on the scheduled dates, but all will be favorably impressed that the publication thinks enough of the advertiser to send a representative to meet in person.

Occasionally it is necessary to cancel a trip due to a shortage of appointments. This is particularly true in New York and Detroit at certain times of the year. Rather than undertake travel that will cost the association more than $125 per meeting, it is more prudent to call back those who have agreed to an appointment, to explain that the trip must be postponed. Those who were unable to meet will never know the trip was cancelled, and the salesperson will still be credited with the attempt. When the trip is rescheduled, those who declined before will go out of their way to arrange an appointment.

The first face-to-face meeting is similar in substance to the first telephone call. Ask intelligent questions before attempting to sell. Even though the answers may be known, advertising personnel, plans, and programs are subject to constant change, and require diligent review. Prior to a sales presentation of the publication's advertising values elicit this information:

- What are your marketing objectives?
- In what publications are you currently advertising?
- Are you considering any others?
- When is the critical planning period?
- Who else should be seen or written at the company and advertising agency?

Understanding the advertiser's marketing objectives is the key to successful selling. Last year the consumer advertiser may have been interested in the 25–45 age group; this year objectives may have shifted to 45–65. The business advertiser who previously tried to cover only middle-management readers who actually buy their products may have discovered through research the importance of top management who must approve each purchase.

After obtaining the necessary information, an advertising salesperson is in an excellent position to demonstrate those particular values that fall within the marketing objectives. Knowing the competition also allows for skillful comparisons of the association publication with other publications, stressing the strengths of the one being sold over any weaknesses of the others.

A salesperson's appearance and demeanor reflect the publication and organization being represented. Most advertisers will never meet anyone else from the magazine or association; when a publication comes up, they will immediately picture the advertising representative whom they have met.

Every personality type will be encountered. Hardened advertising managers with 25 years in the same company have heard every conceivable sales pitch, and many stoics, unless prodded with questions, will listen without making a contribution or revealing their real feelings.

At the other extreme are the "numbers" people. Many media buyers are working in their first jobs at advertising agencies, with too little experience to appreciate the significance of a trade association or other nonprofit organization and their publications' member-readers. Too frequently their primary concern is the magazine's "numbers" (fine-tuned circulation breakdowns and their costs per thousand), according to guidelines given them by the media director or account executive. Being argumentative is fruitless, but negative observations should be refuted with conviction. A weak publication sold with conviction will be more successful than a strong one presented poorly.

Productive sales calls can be conducted in 20 to 30 minutes. Ask questions, present the case within the advertiser's marketing objectives, ask for questions or comments, answer or refute, summarize the publication's values, and exit. Regardless of the tenor of the meeting, whether the advertiser was apathetic or negative, leave each meeting on a warm and friendly note. Brevity, conviction, and warmth will ensure future appointments, and may even result in an order before the second meeting.

Repeat, repeat, repeat the publication's values to each advertiser in follow-up letters, telephone calls, and succeeding sales calls. The competition is stressing their strengths vs. other magazines'; advertisers' memories dim or become confused unless salient distinguishing characteristics are consistently brought to their attention.

Advertising Renewal

After the first insertion order, advertisers continue to require attention and assistance. Offer to send copies of the magazine with their ads to sales managers or distributors to demonstrate their advertising support to the company's marketing efforts. Merchandising copies to key personnel broadens the base of backers within the company. Advertising doubles its value by selling its readers and providing ammunition to the company's marketing staff.

Successful salespeople never take a sale for granted. Values are resold annually, but contact is maintained throughout the year.

Position requests cannot be fulfilled in every issue, but regular advertisers can be given their share of preferable positions with careful rotation. Full-color advertisers request up-front or cover positions, coupon advertisers ask for a right-hand page not backed with another coupon, and small-space advertisers may ask to be placed within a particular department or section of the magazine. Most are reasonable requests; evenhanded treatment with a sympathetic attitude increases the probability of renewal.

Entertaining valued advertisers is no longer essential as it was in previous years. The three martini lunch is a relic of the past, before the health-conscious, more serious business environment of the present. Publications with circulations in the hundreds of thousands or millions, with high advertising rates, are still expected to entertain their customers on a regular basis, but the typical nonprofit magazine salesperson seldom meets the advertiser.

If on a business trip, a business luncheon is the preferable means of entertaining, though not mandatory. It provides a means of relaxing away from the office atmosphere, an opportunity to cement relationships with established or potential advertisers. But the luncheon is not the time for heavy selling.

After one or two years of planned advertising sales, the nonprofit management or publication editor is in a position to consider other options for increasing advertising revenue. Should the magazine be audited? Should outside sales representatives be interviewed?

Considering an Audit

The decision to audit requires thoughtful consideration. It can be disruptive within the association, requiring exact procedures by the circulation and business staff. It is time-consuming and reflects a commitment to be accountable for every subscriber and every copy of the publication.

Many of the largest advertising agencies require an audit. It provides them with consistent measurements of paid subscribers, controlled circulation, newsstand sales, circulation inducements, and renewals. The audit protects them from the few unscrupulous or casual publishers who falsify records or fail to delete subscribers who do not renew.

Agencies also use the audit as an excuse to reduce their work load. By declaring a policy of evaluating only the audited publications, an agency is saying to its clients that there is no need to consider the many other unaudited publications in the same SRDS classification.

When an agency refuses to evaluate an unaudited publication, appeal to the company advertising manager, citing the organization's meticulous record keeping of its members, print orders, and sworn statement to SRDS as sufficient proof of circulation validity. If turned down by the company and the agency, there is no recourse. That company will not advertise until the publication is audited by the Audit Bureau of Circulation (ABC), Business Publishers Audit (BPA), or Magazine Publishers Audit (MPA).

Of the 30 nonprofit publications listed in figures 3–4 and 3–5, only three business and three consumer magazines are unaudited. They are either small-circulation magazines or in a field where most of their competitors are unaudited.

Expense is not a primary factor. The annual cost may vary from three to five pages of advertising revenue. The real questions concern the amount of projected income that would be lost without an audit, and the association's willingness to commit itself to disciplined circulation procedures on a sustained basis to obtain increased revenue. If it can be clearly shown the magazine will attract at least 12 additional four-color pages of advertising annually with an audit, the investment is well worth the commitment.

Considering Outside Representatives

A publication's advertising dollar potential and the association's in-house sales or supervisory capability are ingredients to be considered before contracting with outside sales representatives.

If the dollar potential is minimal, an inexperienced, intelligent person with good work habits can be relied on to manage advertising sales and production materials in-house without outside assistance. This is particularly true of newsletters and small circulation bimonthly magazines.

A monthly magazine with over 25,000 circulation, however, may have sufficient potential to consider outside assistance, even with an experienced advertising manager as a salaried employee.

Many options are available, including these currently in use by nonprofit organizations:

1. A single outside representative firm supervised by the editor or executive director.
2. Salaried advertising manager supervising regional representatives 1,000 miles or more from the association headquarters.
3. Salaried advertising sales director at the home office, regional sales directors in three major cities, and outside representatives in other cities and countries.
4. Contract sales representative with offices in association head-quarters, on a straight commission basis, reporting to the editor or executive director.

There are many association and other nonprofit magazines with the dollar potential to be attractive to a professional representative, though too small to justify personal contact other than direct mail and telephone calls. These reps act as the magazine's advertising office, and are usually located within the same metropolitan area. They also represent other publications, performing these duties on a straight commission basis:

1. Conduct promotional mailings, correspondence, and telephone sales.

2. Manage insertion orders and advertising production materials, and maintain advertising records.
3. Collect from advertisers with overdue invoices.

Associations with broad circulations and high page rates often prefer to combine their sales efforts with an in-house advertising professional who supervises supplemental regional sales representatives. For example, a Washington-based magazine has an advertising sales director who reports to the publisher (executive director) and receives salary and benefits, plus a commission or bonus based on the year's advertising performance. This sales director covers the East Coast from New England to Florida and as far West as St. Louis and Chicago, but contracts with regional representatives in Dallas and Los Angeles for western coverage.

A few of the largest association publications not only have a salaried advertising director, but also have their own salaried regional sales managers in such major markets as New York, Chicago, and Los Angeles. In addition to this staff on their payroll, they have regional outside representatives to cover the remainder of the country and key foreign countries.

A variation of these arrangements is the advertising sales professional on a contract basis but located in the association headquarters building. Office space and travel expenses are negotiated, but the rep is responsible for sales, production materials, and collections, and reimburses the association for postage and telephone costs, working on straight commission from net revenue received after agency discounts.

Commissions, too, are flexible. Most publishers pay 25 percent of the net revenue received on new business for the first 12 months, and 20 percent on advertising that renews. One association offered 20 and 15 percent while reimbursing the first $15,000 in travel expenses. The executive director knew there was a high revenue potential if the magazine were sold aggressively through personal contact; travel reimbursement provided the incentive, since most advertising reps are reluctant to spend their own earnings on travel.

What do outside representatives expect of the nonprofit organization? The willingness to allow them to earn good money. Whether they cover the nation or a region, advertising representatives need an income base from which to build. All running business within their territories should be commissionable, with the possible exception of old, reliable advertisers that have been running each year for the past five or more years.

Some nonprofit publishers believe a new representative should receive commissions strictly on new business brought in. Advertising must be renewed annually; without incentive, representatives will ignore the noncommissionable advertisers, and then both parties lose.

In interviewing outside reps, the executive director or editor interviews those most familiar with the markets presenting the greatest advertising potential. What other magazines do they represent? With a consumer magazine, are they familiar with consumer advertising managers and their agencies in the fields of travel, automotive, and consumer electronics? With a business publication, do they know the major industrial and office equipment manufacturers and their agencies, or the business markets served by the nonprofit's publication?

Which magazines provide their principal sources of income? Will the association's magazine receive equal or greater attention, or will it be given short shrift?

Ad representatives seldom turn down a publication with a page rate of $1,000 or more, for they have little to lose. The extent of their efforts, however, will be motivated by the dollar potential. Before signing an agreement, make a careful reference check of other publishers represented, and a spot-check of advertisers and agencies being covered.

In the agreement, be careful to include all details so as to avoid later disputes. The publisher is expected to provide research; the designing, preparation, and printing of sales materials; and monthly copies of the magazine for media kits, although this, too, is negotiable.

The outside representative normally pays for all other costs in return for the 25 and 20 percent commission, payable after collection.

Although not common practice, it is advisable to insist on these added requirements of the advertising representative: an annual marketing plan, a brief quarterly report, and an annual analysis.

Analysis and Marketing Plan

Regardless of the sales arrangement—whether sold inside, outside, or both—nonprofit management has every right to expect updated reports on sales results and sales efforts based on an annual marketing plan.

Each quarter the sales manager or representative should submit a brief summary of advertising pages and dollars vs. the previous 12-month period:

1st Quarter: Page and dollar gains or losses vs. the previous first quarter.

2nd Quarter: Page and dollar gains or losses vs. the previous six months.

3rd Quarter: Page and dollar gains or losses vs. the previous third quarter, and vs. the previous first nine months.

4th Quarter: Page and dollar gains or losses vs. the previous fourth quarter, and vs. the previous 12-month period.

The annual, or fourth-quarter analysis, becomes even more meaningful when it includes a two-year comparison of advertising pages per issue, average dollars per issue, and—by dividing the dollars by the pages—advertising dollars per page. The dollars-per-page figure should increase even when total advertising revenue declines, since it is a reflection of advertising rate increases.

While it would be extremely helpful to obtain a comprehensive analysis of gains or losses, measuring the advertising in competitive magazines is too arduous a task to request of an outside representative. The advertising sales manager could, however, break down its own advertisers by classifications and make these comparisons with the previous year:

1. Gains and losses by category (travel, office equipment, etc.)
2. New advertisers by category
3. Advertisers that increased pages
4. Advertisers with the same number of pages
5. Advertisers that decreased pages
6. Advertisers from the previous year that dropped out

This type of analysis not only keeps management informed, it signals sudden declines and new opportunities, and provides a basis for the next year's marketing plan.

The annual marketing plan need not be complicated, particularly if it is required of an outside representative. These elements are suggested for the next year's sales planning—month-by-month activities compared with those of the previous year:

1. Sales trips in the past year compared with planned trips for the year ahead
2. Direct mail efforts in the two years
3. Major telephone efforts for convention and special issues
4. Updated research and promotional materials requirements for the year ahead

The annual marketing plan and analysis should be summarized and interpreted in a cover letter to management, along with predictions—if not projections—of the advertising climate ahead.

Advertising is merely one of a nonprofit organization's marketing efforts. Plans and analyses should be closely coordinated with other dues and nondues income-producing activities.

8. Meetings and Conventions

Seminars, roundtables, weekend fly-ins, and conventions are a pleasant combination—definitely of benefit to members, and a major source of nondues revenue for nonprofit organizations, associations, and societies. While the potential advertising revenue from meetings and conventions has been covered, substantial income can also be realized through registration sales, sponsorships, exhibits, and suite sales.

People enjoy meeting with their peers. Overheard at the first annual Disc Jockey Convention in the lobby of the grand old Muehlebach Hotel in Kansas City was this classic comment: "Can you believe it? Everywhere you look—DJs just like us!" It is this sense of excitement that must be conveyed to prospective attendees—librarians and morticians as well as radio personalities. So long as the group has common interests and concerns, members can be enticed by the thought of leaving their daily routines to eat, drink, and share laughs and information with their counterparts.

Registration Sales

The degree of hype depends on the nature of the meeting. One- or two-day seminars seldom justify a major allocation of money to attract registration sales. With careful planning, however, registration sales campaigns can be orchestrated to build to a crescendo on a modest budget.

There are four elements of registration sales planning:

1. direct mail promotion
2. publicity
3. advertising
4. promotional tie-ins

Promotional planning should be initiated at least nine months prior to meetings or conventions. What direct mail pieces will be printed? How many and how much will they cost? How many news stories can be developed, what are the topics, who will write them, and where can they be placed? How about advertising in the association's publications, with other nonprofit publications, and the trades? Can the meetings be tied in with other promotions or other meetings? How can other nonprofit organizations be involved?

Just one note about registration pricing. If nonmembers are permitted to attend, most associations make them pay for it. The additional cost to attend seminars or conventions as a nonmember is a strong inducement to join the organization. The only exception to this two-tiered registration fee are those individuals who are encouraged to attend but who are ineligible for membership. For example, a trade association for companies in an industry should place a high premium on registration fees for employees of eligible nonmember companies, but a modest fee for government agency personnel or students with a shared interest, but ineligible to join.

If it is in the best interests of the organization to encourage their attendance, hold the registration rates within their means. If, however, attendees are potential members, use every inducement, including a major price spread, to encourage their membership.

Direct Mail Promotion. Before promoting a seminar or convention, consider the benefits. Comparable to selling new members, retaining old members, or selling anything of value, analyze the benefits before planning the campaign.

Examine the features that may induce members, nonmembers, and possibly their families, to attend:

1. location
2. sessions

3. speakers
4. entertainment
5. exhibits and suites
6. spouses' program
7. hotel, airline, and car rental discounts

Start with the meeting's location. Although some areas are more attractive than others, every city or resort area has promotable features.

Climate can also be a factor. Meeting and convention planners know how people enjoy winter meetings in Phoenix, Tucson, Palm Springs, Las Vegas, or any of Florida's cities; spring meetings in Washington, D.C., Charleston, Atlanta, New Orleans, Houston, Dallas, and San Antonio; summer meetings in Denver, San Francisco, Seattle, and San Diego; and fall meetings in Boston, New York, Chicago, and St. Louis.

When holding a conference in a city, check first with the local chamber of commerce. What are the city's major attractions? Does it have interesting museums, galleries, or shopping areas? Ask for brochures and photographs—black-and-white, color (four-color separations if they are available), and aerial views. Photos can be used in the direct mail pieces and in the association's publications. Palm trees, ocean vistas, snow-capped mountains, beautiful parks, monuments, and museums are subtle inducements to attend. The same is true of the city's convention hotel. Photographs of the lobby, rooms, suites, bars, restaurants, pool, and health club may also be used in the direct mail promotional materials.

When a meeting is to be located at a resort, confer closely with its salespeople for a thorough description of its facilities and nearby attractions. They too will provide photographs as needed. Golf courses are always photogenic, but do not overlook the tennis courts, swimming pools, bars, and restaurants for those with other recreational inclinations.

Visual materials may trigger a subliminal desire to register, but even these need to be reinforced with reason. Practical questions, too, need attention: "Why should my company or I spend money for registration, airfare, a hotel room and sundry items to attend this function, even though I know I would enjoy it?"

Solid reasons, described in a convincing manner, must be given to members if only to help them rationalize their attendance. "What will I learn? How can this benefit me or my company? Who will I see there?"

Examine the subjects to be discussed. A seminar may revolve around a single subject with great urgency, while a convention may include sessions that cover every phase of a profession or business. A clear statement of the subjects is important, but sell the sizzle with the steak.

Instead of "Marketing Implementation," a session might be titled "Turning a Sales Plan into Action." "How Government Regulations Affect the Industry" could be described as "Loosening the Noose of Federal Regs."

When a professional person or middle-management executive reads a seminar or convention program, the session descriptions must be convincing. They must stand up to scrutiny by those in top management and accounting who approve the expenditure and expense accounts. If the costs are borne by the member, all the more reason to herald an exciting program with substance.

Featured speakers are an added inducement. They may be leaders in the industry, profession, or government. Although their names may not be recognizable, at least their titles should be a drawing attraction. At luncheons and dinners many organizations bring in popular figures from outside the industry—respected journalists, television personalities, actors, controversial figures such as Gordon Liddy or Oliver North, and even well-known comedians.

That brings us to entertainment. At most small meetings and conventions, featured speakers are the *only* entertainment. However, major conventions frequently go beyond speakers to include one or more the following: performing artists, name bands and marching real bands, fireworks or laser shows, rodeos, and barbecues. The mode of entertainment is limited only by the imagination of a P. T. Barnum.

That is sizzle. On a somewhat more serious side, but also entertaining and informative, are conventions that feature exhibits and hospitality suites. To attract attendees to the exhibit floor, associations hold prize drawings and cocktail receptions with strolling musicians and waitresses to move the crowds around the hall. After the meetings and exhibit hours, attendees are encouraged to visit suppliers' hospitality suites in the convention hotels.

Aside from the entertainment aspect, exhibits are definitely a learning experience, often one of the prime reasons for attending a convention. Before registering, prospective attendees should be informed of the types of products and services to be on display, particularly any new technology that is to be introduced at the show.

When the registrants are predominantly male, many associations provide a spouses' program for their wives. Recently the spouse of a female executive attended a spouses' program and was elated with the attention he received from the wives. A major convention can be turned into a reasonable vacation for many couples, since most of the expenses are covered by the attendees' companies. When expenses are paid out of their own pockets, at least they are tax-deductible.

With the assistance of the convention city's chamber of commerce or resort management, any number of events can be scheduled for the spouses' program:

- *Tour of the city*, museums, zoos, aquariums, and unusual residential areas.
- *Luncheons* with fashion shows, interesting speakers, or authors.
- *Tour of the countryside*, such as historic sites outside Boston or the wine country north of San Francisco, with luncheons at country inns.
- *Tennis, golf, and bridge groups*, according to their interests.

Through direct mail the nonprofit organization can rivet its members' attention by dramatizing the location; sell the need to attend by highlighting the sessions and featured speakers; describe the exhibits to be displayed; then stress the entertainment opportunities for members and spouses. The final incentive: discounts. Substantial registration discounts are available to members vs. nonmembers; airline, hotel registration, and car rental discounts are available to all who attend.

The number of direct mail pieces is determined by the meeting size and number of benefits. One large piece should feature all the benefits, along with a registration form. The single brochure may be the only promotional piece required for a roundtable or seminar. Since there are no exhibits, entertainment, or spouses' program, emphasis is on the subject matter, featured speakers, and location.

The same brochure, with varied cover letters, can be sent in two or three mailings to both members and potential members.

Not even the brochure or cover letter are considered necessary by some associations. The American Logistics Association, announcing a two-and-one-half-day seminar, merely mails two single 8½″ x 11″ sheets folded in half and stapled, to both members and nonmembers. One side of one sheet presents the roundtable program, with descriptions of the sessions and speakers. A second side provides general information on hotel reservations with discounts, airline discounts, member and nonmember registration fees, and other registration information. On the back side is a complete registration form. When the two pages are folded and stapled, the outer panels highlight the roundtable, date, and location on one side and the mailing label, return address, and indicia on the other.

If the organization is holding a series of regional seminars, it is advisable to include all of the dates and locations in a single promotional brochure. For example, assume there will be six regional seminars over a two-month period in Boston, Washington, Atlanta, Chicago, Denver, and Los Angeles. Members in Pennsylvania and New York may choose to tie in the seminar with other business in Washington, or combine the seminar with a New England vacation. A member in Dallas may choose Chicago or Denver depending on timing conflicts or the desired combination of business with business or business with pleasure.

For major conventions, the direct mail campaign should be staged over a four-month period. Accompanying the basic brochure, smaller enclosures can extol the convention city or resort, featured speakers, entertainment, spouses' program, and travel discounts.

Cover letters to members and nonmembers can vary their appeals. The former might be more personal, such as "Share Your Insights with Fellow Members," "Participate in Your Organization's Head-to-Head Event" or "Learn, Make Friends, and Enjoy!"

Letters to prospective members have a dual goal—attend and join, with less stress on entertainment. Use phrases such as "Come Join With Us," "It's Your Industry (or Profession), Too," "Just One of the Many Benefits." If nonmembers really believe they will benefit by attending the association's meetings and conventions, the heavily discounted registration rate for members can be the final incentive to join.

If an association has a telemarketing operation, it pays to concentrate calls on potential attendees who live within a day's drive of the convention site. Their transportation costs are considerably less, just one more incentive to attend.

Whether the emphasis is on information or entertainment or even cost, all direct mail letters, promotion pieces, and telephone calls must convey a sense of excitement. After all, if the aura is staid and instructional, why not stay home and simply order the cassettes?

Publicity. Articles about upcoming seminars and conventions are an effective means of inciting and sustaining interest. Publicity reaches out to members through the nonprofit organization's newsletter or magazine, and to nonmembers through the trade press and related organization publications. There is only one drawback—no registration form. Display advertising with registration reply coupons will offset this limitation in house organs, but may be too expensive to place in other publications.

Because of this lack of a reply device, include a fax and toll-free number, if possible, in every article submitted to outside editors. It should be written into the body of the copy, then repeated at the end in bold face:

FOR REGISTRATION INFORMATION, CALL OR FAX _____ AT (800) 338-8000 OR (604) 963-1221, AND SPECIFY THE ANNUAL CONVENTION IN KEO-KUK.

Due to space limitations, editors may cut the last line, ending with the numbers, or may be constrained to drop the final two or three paragraphs. If the toll-free number is retained in the body of the piece, however, a means for spontaneous response is preserved.

Timing is important. Monthly magazine editors prefer to have materials two or three months before the publication date. If an annual convention is held in April, attempt to place articles in February or March issues; April may be too late to attract registrants. Since most February issues are closed by the end of December, and

March issues by late January, articles should be submitted no later than early November and December. Weekly and semimonthly magazines have shorter lead time, while bimonthlies require more advance planning than monthlies. The crucial point is to know in advance the closing dates of each publication, and provide editors with sufficient leeway.

For best results, call each editor *before* submitting a press release or article. Stress the relevance of the meeting or convention to that publication's readers. Ask for the preferred format. Would the editor be interested in interviewing one of the organization's executives? Would they prefer a submitted Q-and-A interview? Perhaps a news article attuned to the readers' interests would better fit the format. Request as much space as possible; pare it down according to the editor's constraints.

In other than the nonprofits' own publications, seminars seldom achieve more than one article or item in issues preceding the event. A major convention, however, could result in this procession of valuable publicity, particularly if the leading trade magazine in the field is a weekly:

1. Major article about the convention
2. Program listing—sessions, speakers, and events
3. Interview with the organization president on the future of the industry or profession
4. List of exhibitors and description of exhibits

Trade magazines sell advertising to exhibitors. If they are assured in advance that they will be given detailed exhibitor information just before the convention, editors and publishers will look more favorably on giving the convention full news treatment. They may print a major article, list the program, and possibly interview the president, spreading the coverage over a period of weeks or months prior to the event.

Newsletters and magazines owned by related nonprofit organizations will also give fair treatment to meetings and conventions, if there is reciprocation. Articles and items can be exchanged, as well as advertising, all subject to negotiation with sister organizations. They are important, for their readers are potential registrants and may be potential members.

Readership studies usually reveal what publications are read by the organization's members. A chemical engineering society, for example, knows many of its members read several chemical magazines and a leading engineering tabloid. They may be commercial trade publications or published by related nonprofit organizations. Regardless, publicity in them will result in additional registrants and, in turn, more new members.

The most obvious source of publicity is in-house publications. Upcoming meetings and seminars should be covered in every issue for three months preceding the meeting dates, and conventions treated as a developing news story for the previous four or five months.

Each of the direct mail elements is a possible story in itself. Write about the city or resort where meetings are to be held; describe the sessions and invited speakers; highlight new technologies, new products, and services to be exhibited; prepare feature stories on the entertainment and spouses' program; mention the hotel, airline, and car rental companies with the discounts they offer registrants.

After years of pulling together the myriad details involved in planning meetings and conventions, it is understandable that nonprofit staff members may groan at the thought of going through the cycle once again each year. It should not be perceived as an onerous routine by the association's members, however. When that occurs, they will no longer attend. Call it showbiz, call it hype, but when meetings no longer appear both informative and exciting, attendance will decline. If exhibitors are involved, they too will drop out, since their major investment demands high attendance rates on the exhibit floor.

Direct mail conveys excitement; well-planned, consistent publicity sustains it. Life is not always what is; life is what it is perceived to be.

Advertising. Even though favorable publicity incites and sustains interest in nonprofit meetings and conventions, it cannot ask for the order. Registration sales advertising is expected to explain the benefits of attending, and to provide a means for a positive decision. Full- or half-page ads placed in other publications should be informative as well as attractive. Since most readers will be nonmembers, advertising should explain the meeting's purpose, describe the sessions and speakers, and summarize both tangible and intangible benefits for registrants.

In addition to a registration form, provide a fax and toll-free phone number for those who can make an immediate decision or require more information. Credit card orders are a convenience for individuals; companies may be billed with the understanding that fees must be paid before on-site registration.

In the nonprofit's own publications, where the meeting or convention is the subject of an article in the same issue, only the registration form and related information need appear in the ad.

One very successful association convention registration form is cited, with a note of caution. Not every organization has a convention so popular that it is in a position to impose all these regulations, charges, and penalties. This appeared in a January issue house publication advertisement for a convention to be held in mid-April (a front-page article described the convention in great detail):

REGISTRATION FORM AND INSTRUCTIONS

REGISTRATION INSTRUCTIONS:

To *register*,

- Send completed registration form and full payment of registration fee.
- **Before March 8** you may register by phone or by fax. Registration must be received by March 8 to be included on the pre-registration list.
- **Delegates eligible to attend at member rate:** Members; associate members; military personnel, clergy, students; reps of charitable organizations; government personnel; representatives of educational institutions.
- **If pre-registration is received by February 22:** Credentials will be mailed in advance; to receive badge holder and program bring your credential packet to the convention hotel registration desk; international registrants (except for Canadians) must pick up their registration packets at the convention hotel.
- **Spouses** will receive complimentary badge only; function tickets purchased separately; badge admits spouse to meetings and exhibit halls.
- **On-site registration:** Late registrants must register on site at

$50 more than the preregistration rates; payable by cash, check, VISA, American Express, MasterCard.

- **Credentials packet** includes: name badge and plastic imprinted card; two luncheon tickets; tour bus ticket (if purchased); spouse's badge (complimentary); request for refund form.
- **Registration hours:** Saturday, April 3, 4:00-8:00 pm; Sunday, April 4, 8:00 am-5:00 pm; Thursday, April 8, 8:00 am-1:00 pm.
- **Registration changes:** A $50 fee will be charged to change or replace lost badges; lost badges/tickets will NOT be replaced free of charge.
- **Refunds:** Complete a Request for Refund Form (included in packet); refund requests will be processed 6–8 weeks after the convention, not on-site; there will be a $100 administrative fee; credentials packet MUST be returned with request for refund form; entertainment; tours, and additional meal tickets are nonrefundable.

REGISTRATION FORM:

- **Personal:** Name, title, company, address, city, state, country, zip code, telephone and fax numbers; exact name and information as you wish it to appear on your and spouse's badge; primary interest, primary job function, and primary business (check one only).
- **Advance registration fees (on-site, add $50):**

Member rate	$250
Nonmember rate	$550
*Additional meal function tickets	$ 35
*Closing entertainment tickets	$ 35
'Bus tour tickets	$ 20
*Nonrefundable	

ANY DELINQUENT DUES MUST BE PAID PRIOR TO REGISTRATION

- **Method of Payment:** Check; American Express, MasterCard, VISA.
- **Other information requested:**

> **Membership status:** Member, Associate Member, Non-member (check to receive membership information).
> Check conventions attended in past two years.
> Check those you plan to attend in next two years.

This in-house publication advertisement offers no description of the convention itself; the front-page article carries the full burden of enticing its readers to attend.

When exchanging ads with other nonprofit publications, or placing paid advertising with the trade press, attempt to run them in the same issues with articles concerning the meetings. Request that the ad be placed *after* the article and, if necessary, in the back of the publication. Very little mileage can be gained from an up-front position before the article, even though the ad itself summarizes the reasons for attending. Allow the publicity to inform and stimulate interest; use the advertisement, with registration form, as the clincher.

The registration marketing package is complete: a series of direct mail offers to controlled lists of members and nonmembers and publicity and advertising in publications owned by the organization, other related nonprofits, and trade press known to be read by current and potential members.

What other means are available to increase meeting registration revenue? Look for tie-in possibilities with the membership department and other nonprofit organizations.

Promotional Tie-ins. When there is a significant spread between the member and nonmember registration fees, an appealing convention is a tremendous asset to the nonprofit organization's membership department.

Besides the incentive to retain current members, nonmembers inclined to join or attend the convention may sign up just to be eligible for the greatly discounted registration fee. The registration marketing program, with its well-planned combination of direct mail, publicity, and advertising, should have a positive effect on membership.

The National Association of Broadcasters (NAB) has carried this a step further. By offering a trial membership period at a discounted membership rate, it has found the convention to be the greatest incentive for converting trial members to regular ones.

Timing is essential. Five months before the annual convention (to be held in Washington, D.C.), letters soliciting members offer a three-month NAB trial membership prorated with a 25 percent discount off the regular rate.

After signing up, trial members receive a postcard every two weeks, depicting the White House, Capitol building, or other familiar Washington scenes in front, and a description of many membership benefits on the back. The attractive postcards ensure readership. The frequent mailings reinforce the abundance of NAB member benefits. Trial members are encouraged to participate in association activities and avail themselves of the generous member discounts.

The trial period expires just a few weeks prior to the annual convention. Letters and calls from the membership department repeat the benefits and stress the convention registration discount if they decide to continue their membership—at the full member rate.

NAB reports a 91 percent conversion rate on its first attempt at this trial offer. Since this is an innovation, it is too soon to determine how many months or years members gained in this manner will continue at the full rate. Nevertheless, it is a low-risk, high-return offer. It adds new members at barely 6 percent off the annual membership dues over a three-month period, costs very little, and attracts more registrants for the convention. Without the significant registration discount for members vs. nonmembers, however, the tie-in campaign would be considerably less successful.

Another convention tie-in possibility is cooperating with related nonprofit groups, encouraging them to hold their meetings just before or after the convention. Smaller organizations with common interests or concerns may not have the means to hold a convention of their own. Knowing that many of their members will be attending, it is to their advantage to tie in with a state or national convention where they can conduct their own business or special functions.

For example, assume the American Bar Association holds its annual convention and a subgroup, the trial lawyers, tie in their meeting the day before. This could also apply to state or regional organizations. The Nebraska Bar Association, for example, might tie in its meetings with the national association convention held in San Diego.

Tie-ins with related nonprofit groups provide dual opportunities.

Convention registration sales can be increased, and all organizations involved stand to gain new members.

Mailing lists can be exchanged. In the case cited, the national group might exchange its list of trial lawyers with the trial lawyers' membership list. Or it could exchange its list of members in Nebraska with the Nebraska lawyers' list.

Also possible are exchanges of publicity and advertising among the large and smaller organizations. The trial and Nebraska lawyers' newsletters could feature the national convention in articles and house ads, in an attempt to persuade their members to attend their meetings before or after the convention.

The national organization would also mention the tie-in meetings in its publications, and even exchange advertising with the smaller groups. Since all those on direct mail lists or who read the publications are attorneys, they are either current or potential members of the national association.

Through direct mail promotion, publicity, advertising, tie-ins with related organizations, and telemarketing (when available), meeting and convention registration sales revenue can be an important factor in a nonprofit organization's overall marketing program.

To offset the growing costs identified with seminars and conventions, however, another marketing method is being employed by many nonprofits—the sale of sponsorships.

Selling Sponsorships

Local, state, and national nonprofits should consider soliciting sponsorships to defray the considerable expense of their gatherings. Those without revenue from exhibits or advertising often find it particularly difficult to cover meeting costs. Registration fees may barely equal the expenses, if all goes well, but the sale of sponsorships can help make meetings profitable.

Luncheons, dinners, coffee breaks, and receptions are frequently sponsored by companies looking for ways to be identified with the goals of nonprofits.

At the local level, banks and insurance agencies are not insulted when approached as sponsors. They gain favorable exposure, and may eventually benefit even more directly.

In a small, isolated community in Colorado, for example, the local chamber of commerce decided the town should have a cattle sales barn. Instead of shipping cattle to a city some distance away, area ranchers could bring their livestock to the town to be fattened, auctioned, or shipped to Denver. The chamber invited ranchers to a dinner meeting in the town's only hotel. The local bank sponsored the dinner. After a hearty 16-ounce blood-red prime rib, Idaho potato, giant salad, and two or three water glasses of bonded bourbon, the ranchers volunteered to contribute to the construction of a barn, covering the down payment. The town provided the land and the bank financed the balance.

On a much more sophisticated basis, this example is being applied by colleges and hospitals with expansion plans, where alumni or community leaders are invited to sponsored luncheons and dinners (covered under special events fund raising).

The Wolf Trap Foundation for the Performing Arts in Vienna, Virginia, offers summer entertainment in a beautiful wooded setting. It has both a covered stage and orchestra section, and a vast lawn area where attendees can picnic before and during the varied performances. Inside its handsome brochure Wolf Trap announces:

Someplace Special, Giant Gourmet is Wolf Trap's Official 1991 Picnic Caterer. For great performance picnics, call (703) 448-0800.

That, too, is a form of sponsorship, with an implied endorsement combined with convenience.

Trade associations have many business firms more than willing to sponsor meeting functions. Even one-day seminars usually include a luncheon and two coffee breaks, and often conclude with a dinner or are preceded by a continental breakfast. Each can be sponsored with generous credit mentioned in the program along with a placard at the event.

Most two-day meetings include one or more receptions for attendees. A reception with open bar, hors d'oeuvres, or a buffet can be extremely expensive. Some include entertainment, adding to the expense.

Sponsors of major events naturally expect more than a favorable mention in the association's newsletter and program. An executive of the sponsoring company, alongside the organization's president or executive director, may be permitted to greet attendees as they enter. The company's staff sales representatives may also be near the entrance or mingle with guests, wearing badges that identify them as "hosts" of the function.

Nonprofit management people, especially those not concerned with revenue-producing activities, may take a dim view of commercialization of their meetings. Although company-sponsored events are normally conducted with dignity, it is really an issue that should be decided by the members. If members strongly object, so be it. It is their organization. Members may be willing to pay higher registration fees or discontinue certain functions rather than have sponsored events, but that is seldom the case.

Rather than having it appear as if a sponsoring company is buying its way in, nonprofits can dilute the effect by rotating sponsors or by having several sponsored events. Sponsors cannot expect or demand a quid pro quo; their benefits should be limited to gaining a higher profile with the membership, identifying them as generous contributors to the success of the organization.

Are sponsors expected to pay the entire cost of their functions? When expenses are relatively reasonable, a nonprofit can ask the sponsor to cover the cost or simply charge a flat rate that may exceed actual expenses. For major events, however, a sponsor may pay for only a portion of the total.

Here are a few examples of nonprofit functions and likely rates being asked of their sponsors:

Sponsored Functions	Number in Attendance	Sponsor's Commitment
Regional Roundtables	35	
Continental Breakfast and Coffee Break		$2,500
Luncheon		$2,500

Sponsored Functions	Number in Attendance	Sponsor's Commitment
One-Day Seminar	50	
Luncheon and two Coffee Breaks		$5,000
Weekend Fly-in	60	
Opening Reception the night before and Continental Breakfast		$5,000
Coffee Break		$2,000
Luncheon		$5,000
Board Meeting	75	
Reception the night before		$5,000
Convention	3,000	
Opening Reception		$25,000

A flat charge, designed to cover the anticipated costs, is placed on most events. One association combines continental breakfast and the morning coffee break for sale to a single sponsor for $2,500, and the luncheon is covered by another sponsor for $2,500. These are regional roundtables, where different sponsors pick up the tab within each region.

Another organization held a one-day seminar, with only one sponsor who was charged $5,000 to cover the expenses of the luncheon and two coffee breaks.

There are three sponsors for a weekend fly-in with 60 attendees. One covers the opening reception the evening before plus the continental breakfast the next morning. A second company sponsors the coffee break, and a third sponsors the luncheon. There is no afternoon coffee break. Total revenue from sponsorships is $12,000, more than enough to cover actual expenses.

Major convention events can seldom be paid in full by sponsors. A welcoming reception for 3,000 delegates actually costs an association $70,000, but the sponsor is asked to pay only $25,000. There is no open bar; attendees receive one drink ticket in their registration package, and purchase tickets at the cash bar for additional beverages.

What does the sponsor receive in return for $25,000? The reception is named after the company sponsor. With 3,000 registrants streaming through several doors it is impossible to greet attendees as they enter, but salespeople circulate among the guests and offer extra drink tickets to their better customers and prospects. The association provides the sponsor with 100 drink tickets, and special reserved tables at luncheon and dinner functions. Only the tables are reserved; those seated at the tables must be registered with their own paid function tickets. The sponsor is willing to settle for prestige and recognition, not a bad combination.

Featured speakers are also sponsored when they are essential to the success of a meeting and their fees are more than the budget permits. For example, when a noted research expert and author charged $20,000 to address a large meeting of industry executives, a research firm closely associated with the author's subject sponsored the event. The sponsor's staff people did not speak, but the company received recognition for bringing the speaker and covering the expense.

At the other extreme, there are small companies that may not be able to afford the cost to exhibit their products or services, or to sponsor events. One association convention provides a room for these small companies to give presentations to interested attendees. For a one-hour presentation they are charged $500, and they are listed in the convention program.

Another sponsorship innovation is a registration bag with the convention logo and the sponsor's logo on the bag. Inside are 20 inserts or fliers sold to suppliers for $1,500 each. The primary sponsor pays for the bags plus $1 per registrant for stuffing, and the inserts are covered by each of the 20 sponsors. Since the inserts refer to products on exhibit, there is a waiting list for sponsors.

For a nonprofit organization to be successful in selling sponsorships, the key is to place the right sponsor with the right event, according to one association executive. To do that, find the staff member who best understands the sales problems and the relationship of suppliers to the organization's members.

That may be the person in the membership department who works with associate members, the advertising salesperson who is familiar with the needs of advertisers, or an exhibit salesperson who knows and understands exhibitors. Better yet, it may be an association executive who has come from and knows the industry or profession served, identifies the proper types of sponsors for each function, and turns that information over to those in charge of the events.

Sponsorship is an acceptable practice as long as it is understood that the organization is not beholden to sponsors other than to provide recognition. In no way should there be an implication of endorsement, any more than a magazine implies endorsement of its advertisers.

9. Exhibits and Hospitality Suites

There are associations whose exhibit income exceeds membership revenue. With many, exhibit space is reserved two or three years in advance. That is a favorable position to be in, for it enables these organizations to be fully staffed to serve all their members' needs, from government experts to economists.

But how does a local, statewide, or small national nonprofit enter the exhibit business? Members who have been attending conventions for many years may object to commercializing their meetings. Exhibits may be considered a distraction to the serious nature of the business at hand.

Twenty years ago the National League of Cities (NLC) faced this problem. The league's meeting attendees are elected mayors and city council members from small towns to major cities. Meetings are extremely serious where they hammer out, after heated discussion and debate, resolutions working with state and federal government agencies.

The NLC board of directors decided to experiment with exhibits by restricting them to nonprofit public interest groups only, and then gauging the reactions of its members. The convention hotel auditorium was set aside for nonprofit exhibitors to sell memberships, books, reports, and other products and urban affairs services.

An exhibit management firm agreed to manage the floor at a very reasonable fee, with the understanding that it would charge considerably more in subsequent years if commercial exhibits were added.

The nonprofit exhibitors paid only for renting tables, chairs, carpets, and wastebaskets, but were not charged for floor space.

As expected, the exhibit was a somber affair; dignified, but not too imaginative. Nevertheless, attendance was high, and the exhibitors were delighted.

A follow-up study of attendees asked the elected officials whether they would like to continue exhibits at future conventions. Surprisingly, they were not only in favor of exhibits, but they expressed the desire for commercial exhibits as well.

The second year NLC retained the exhibit management firm to manage the exhibit hall, and the contract publisher of its magazine, *Nation's Cities*, to manage exhibit sales on a commission basis.

Using its own research for advertisers on the purchasing habits of city officials, *Nation's Cities* brought in 80 commercial exhibitors. Nonprofits were also invited to attend, this time at a special lower rate. Floor attendance that year was higher than the previous year. Not even the nonprofits objected to paying for their space, since the commercial exhibits livened the atmosphere, bringing municipal officials back to the floor on more than one occasion.

By contracting out both exhibit management and sales, the National League of Cities added substantial annual revenue without consuming valuable staff time.

Many statewide organizations also have annual meetings with exhibits, but on a smaller scale. They reserve one or more large rooms adjoining meeting rooms in the convention hotel, and provide tables for their exhibitors. Neither outside management nor sales effort is required. There are always companies in the state anxious to sell a nonprofit's members, and regional sales representatives of large national firms who also want to attend. Exhibits provide them the opportunity to meet with regular and potential customers.

Selecting an Exhibit Management Firm

Most nonprofit organizations with large memberships require the assistance of a reputable exhibit management firm. The only alternative is to add someone to staff who has years of experience in working with hotel and exhibit hall management, labor unions, security personnel, and company exhibitors.

Most exhibit firms are capable of selling the exhibit space, but they also manage the operation, with these responsibilities:

1. Inspect the exhibit hall,
2. Prepare a map of the exhibit floor with numbered booths,
3. Contract with a supplier to provide booth materials, furniture, and labor for exhibitors to rent and install,
4. Prepare exhibitor kits for ordering draping, carpets, furniture, telephones, etc., and spelling out rules and regulations for exhibitors,
5. Sell exhibit space by direct mail and telephone,
6. Assign booth spaces,
7. Manage the exhibit floor and security personnel.

Except for exhibit sales, which can be conducted in-house or in conjunction with the exhibit management firm, all of these steps require experienced people with qualifications outside the realm of most nonprofit organization personnel. They must be sensitive to the needs of the association and its exhibitors, yet tough enough to be respected by the hotel staff, laborers, and security people working on the exhibit floor.

The exhibit manager should work closely with the association's convention planners at the very beginning, including site selection, when possible. This means inspecting the convention hotel or convention center where exhibits will be displayed. How many booths will a facility hold? Is it limited or expandable? Where are the freight entrances? Are they adequate for large equipment? If not, is there space outside the hall available for heavy equipment too large for the exhibit floor?

How much space is needed by the association for rest areas, booths, and special functions such as prize drawings, bars, and food facilities? Where will the exhibit manager and furniture rental supplier be located?

What about security considerations? How many entrances and fire exits are there to be covered? How many security people are required during exhibit hours and when the area is closed?

With all of this in mind, the exhibit manager can prepare a proposed map of the exhibit area, marking off and numbering the exhibit booths in an 8' x 10' or 10' x 10' sequence. Many exhibitors will rent two to four adjacent booths to accommodate their products and personnel. Aisle space is also important, as it allows traffic to flow easily from one area to another while ensuring that attendees don't overlook booths located in the far corners of the exhibit area.

Before the map is distributed to prospective exhibitors, the association's convention staff must study it carefully to be certain its own space needs are met and those areas are blocked off. The exhibit manager, working closely with the local supply rental firm, then prepares an exhibitor kit with detailed instructions and an order form.

The kit explains what the convention will provide each booth, such as draperies, railings, company identification placards, etc., and what the exhibitors must rent. Draped tables, carpets, chairs, and other items are available in varied sizes and colors.

Exhibitors invariably have a thousand questions. The kit should provide answers to all of these along with instructions, including the precise timing for set up and tear down, since exhibitors are not permitted to do either while the exhibit area is open.

Spaces are assigned on a first-come, first-served basis. First, second, and third booth space preferences are sent in with a check as down payment. If none of the spaces is available, the exhibit firm or salesperson calls the exhibitor to negotiate another location.

Selecting the right firm to meet the nonprofit's needs is a painstaking, methodical process. Attend two or three conventions that are not directly competitive, but similar in terms of the exhibitors they attract. Talk with their exhibit managers; as a prospective client, an association executive will be given full treatment.

Observe them at work. Are they pleasant but firm? If not, they will be unable to cope with the demands made on them and demands they must make on those who report to them. Talk with exhibitors. What do they think of the exhibit management? Is the manager sensitive to their needs? Will the exhibitors return next year?

Try to find the manager who has established a good relationship with prospective exhibitors, one whom they respect. Then, rather than go to competitive bids, attempt to negotiate a fair one-year contract.

Negotiations will be based on the percentage of expected gross revenue from exhibit rentals, and that will vary considerably. If negotiations reach an impasse, ask the exhibit firm to recommend another organization best suited to meet the association's requirements. That should break the stalemate, but if not, another firm recommended will probably be reliable, since reputations are extremely important in that closed fraternity.

Exhibit sales may be a factor in negotiating the contract, since the exhibit firm will receive a commission on sales if that is included in the agreement. If the association has strong in-house sales personnel who work on a day-to-day basis with prospective exhibitors, sales control should remain with the nonprofit. As a possible compromise, reach an agreement to share the total sales effort. Specify which associate member or advertiser lists the association will cover, and give the exhibit firm free rein to contact all other companies.

Before reaching a final agreement, specify the individual who will be in charge of the exhibit floor. If the exhibit firm has several managers, be certain the manager assigned has been closely observed and is fully capable of working with all of the people who will be involved.

In-house Exhibit Sales

Selling exhibit space is not as difficult as selling memberships or advertising. To bring exhibitors back year after year, however, requires more patience and understanding.

The prospect lists must be well defined, specific information is required for direct mail promotion, and telephone follow-ups are routine. Once sold, exhibitors will attempt to negotiate the booth assignment, and many will be quite vocal concerning every detail on the exhibit floor.

If exhibit sales are conducted within the nonprofit organization, who should be responsible? Ordinarily, the choice is evident—the person who works most closely with companies selling products and services to its members.

An association or society with associate members usually has someone in the membership department who acts as a liaison with them.

In small organizations it may be the membership director, but someone in membership is responsible for working with associate members.

Nonprofits with magazines or other advertising vehicles are in contact with potential exhibitors, since advertisers, too, sell products and services to their members. The person in charge of advertising sales is another logical candidate for exhibit sales. If there is an outside sales representative firm, it may be willing to sell exhibit space in addition to advertising, also on a straight commission basis.

A nonprofit with both associate members and advertisers could arrange to have the membership and advertising departments share exhibit sales responsibilities. That can work very well, provided that only one person is put in charge. For example, an associate membership director could work exclusively with associate members, delegating the remaining prospects to the advertising department or rep firm. In that case, booth assignments should be made by the associate membership director working in conjunction with the exhibit management firm. That would serve to protect the interests of associate members.

Many associations make it difficult to become exhibitors without first joining as associate members. Either the rental price spread per square foot is so great between members and nonmembers as to encourage membership, or there is simply a policy that all exhibitors must be members. Under those circumstances, it is usually better to have a membership person in charge of exhibit sales.

Who does the selling is not as critical as who assigns the spaces and takes care of exhibitors on the floor.

Targeted Lists. Who are the most logical prospects to exhibit? All companies that sell or service the nonprofit's members are potential exhibitors, but those with existing exhibit budgets are the primary targets.

It is suggested that lists be examined in this order:

1. exhibitors at related nonprofit organization conventions;
2. associate members and potential associate members; and
3. current and potential advertisers.

There will be considerable overlapping of companies within these lists. For that reason, start with those companies already committed to exhibiting. They have exhibit budgets, personnel, and standard exhibits.

Many advertisers seldom exhibit; many exhibitors seldom advertise. All companies, however, closely observe their competitors, particularly the largest exhibitors with whom they compete.

Exhibit salespeople should attend conventions with members similar to their own. The National League of Cities sent its magazine editor and publisher to conventions on law enforcement, mass transportation, and public works. Frequently, these organizations had an exhibit booth on the floor where they exhibited the magazine, special reports, and other publications.

The editor attended meetings, gathering pertinent materials for the magazine, and the publisher worked the exhibit floor. Both talked with exhibitors, discussing their problems and simply getting to know them. Those exhibitors were the key to NLC's later success in selling its own convention, for they had exhibit budgets.

When major exhibitors at other conventions are also associate members, the sales task is less complicated. They know and understand the organization, its purpose, and its members. And they are eligible for the member discount rate.

Each convention has a directory of exhibitors, with company names, addresses, phone and fax numbers, and frequently the person in charge of the exhibit. These directories of conventions by related organizations should be placed on computer for direct mail promotion and follow-up calls.

Each exhibitor directory list should be checked against the nonprofit's own associate member and advertiser lists. From that screening process emerges the priority list—those who have exhibit budgets and are associate members or advertisers.

Companies interested in selling products or services to an association's members have three avenues open to them: they can join as associate members to be identified with the organization, they can advertise in its publications, they can exhibit at its convention.

Current and prospective associate member lists are available from the membership department. The same is true of the advertising department with its lists of advertisers and potential advertisers.

In terms of priorities, there are now six direct mail lists:

1. Exhibitors at related conventions that are also associate members or advertisers
2. Other exhibitors at related conventions
3. Associate members
4. Advertisers
5. Potential associate members
6. Potential advertisers

These lists can be cleaned to eliminate duplication, but—if the names are on computer—it is probably less expensive to mail to all the names.

The first three lists deserve the greatest attention. Known exhibitors and associate members that are not exhibitors should be targeted with more mailings, and contacted directly by telephone and, when possible, in person. Current and potential advertisers and potential associate members should receive at least two mailings, but only advertisers need be phoned.

Although the lists mentioned are based on large national conventions, the principles are the same for local, county, and statewide meetings of nonprofit organizations that accept exhibits.

Smaller nonprofits may simply set up card or dinner tables in the hotel to rent to exhibitors. Instead of attending large conventions, the staff can ask their members to send them exhibitor directories when they attend. They can also ask members for lists of their major equipment and service suppliers, with their names, addresses, and phone numbers.

Members of small nonprofits tend to be more cooperative with the paid staff than do members of large associations. In addition to providing lists of their suppliers, many members who are closely identified with the organization may volunteer to follow up the direct mail effort by calling companies they buy from. Members who have personal relationships with prospective exhibitors can be of tremendous assistance in adding to their organization's revenue.

Before any personal contact is initiated, however, accurate targeted lists are essential to the direct mail effort. Nothing should precede direct mail.

Direct Mail Promotion. Unlike promotional materials sent to potential registrants, exhibitors' direct mail is expected to be more informative than exciting.

National exhibitors may prefer Las Vegas to Cleveland; local exhibitors may prefer St. Louis to Jefferson City. However, location is not a major factor. Nor do exhibitors concern themselves with the subjects of the sessions or the quality of the speakers or entertainment, as long as a large number of regular and potential customers will be in attendance.

Exhibitors are interested in:

- *Analysis of last year's convention attendees*—number, titles, or professions.
- *Member purchasing study*—equipment and services bought in the past two years and expected to be bought in the next two years.
- *Exhibit hall map*—with numbered booths, clearly marked aisles, entrances, and reserved areas.
- *Exhibit hours and special attractions on the floor*—prize drawings, luncheons, receptions, or other events to attract attendees to the exhibit area.
- *Order form*—booth selection, payment schedule, rules, and regulations for exhibitors.

Except for the order form, all the information required could be printed on a single large black-and-white or color brochure. If the budget is limited, not even the brochure is necessary; type the information on both sides of regular stationery and staple them. The content is what counts. Interested exhibitors will read everything sent very carefully, for a considerable investment is at stake.

Exhibitors need to know who attends, and whether they are in a position to recommend or approve a purchase. How many attended the meeting or convention last year? What are their titles or positions—top management, middle management, professionals, or self-employed? Are they buyers or tire kickers? At the very least, will their recommendations be taken seriously by those who do make or approve the purchasing decisions?

In most cases, this information can be taken from the previous year's registration forms filled out by attendees, since titles or professions are usually requested.

Purchasing information may be available from the organizations' publications that sell advertising. Although advertisers are also interested in readership information, they, too, need to know the members' buying habits.

If not available, an nth name purchasing study of members is easily conducted. Type the questionnaire on a single sheet of the organization's stationery using both sides if necessary, have a descriptive introductory paragraph explaining the study to members, and list the services and equipment after this question:

Please check any of the following that you have purchased in the past two years or plan to buy in the next two years:

	Bought in the Past Two Years	*Plan to Buy in the Next Two Years*
Equipment		
_____	_____	_____
_____	_____	_____
_____	_____	_____
Services		
_____	_____	_____
_____	_____	_____
_____	_____	_____

Conclude the study with a sentence asking them to return the questionnaire as quickly as possible in the enclosed postage-paid reply envelope, and thank them for their time.

Since exhibitors are not as fussy about research methods as advertisers, there need be no concern about the number of returns or percent who reply. Just cut off the study after two or three weeks and use the actual number of returns at that time as the base for determining percentages. If the proportion who buy appears to be low, wait another two or three weeks for additional returns and refigure the results. After that length of time, any stragglers will not alter the findings.

There are periods just before, during, or after a recession when members buy very little or do not plan to buy very much. If this is the first study of its kind, one might be justified in releasing only the higher set of figures, since it is proprietary research. However, a true picture of past and future purchases on a historical basis is extremely useful to exhibitors. If repeated every other year, the study becomes a valuable marketing tool.

For example, take an exhibitor of office copiers. Two years ago, 21 percent of the nonprofit's members reported they had purchased or leased a copier in the past two years, but only 14 percent said they planned to obtain a copier in the next two years. This year, 23 percent report they actually bought or leased a copier in the past two years, and 18 percent say they plan to obtain a copier in the next two years.

From this the exhibitor can deduct that while only 14 percent planned to buy two years ago, because of breakdowns, obsolescence, or the need for additional copiers, nearly one out of four (23 percent) actually bought or leased a copier.

Since 18 percent plan to obtain a copier in the next two years, copier firms can expect even more than one-quarter to be in the market in the two years ahead. This type of solid information endears a nonprofit organization to marketers who both exhibit and advertise.

A floor plan of the exhibit area, marked with numbered booths, is an essential element of the direct mail package to exhibitors. The exhibit management firm will provide the plan (if such a firm is involved). If not, it must be drawn by in-house staff with the assistance of hotel or meeting place personnel. Entrances, fire exits, and aisles should be clearly delineated, to enable exhibitors to gauge the traffic flow.

The exhibitors' information packet contains hours and days the exhibit area will be open, and any special events to be held there. Smaller meetings are not able to schedule special events in the exhibit area, but for trade association conventions, such events are a necessity. They influence the number of attendees and demonstrate the association's recognition of its exhibitors and their contribution to the success of the convention. There may be many registrants, but if they are not attracted to the exhibit area, a convention can be a disaster for exhibitors. The extent of their investment necessitates a reasonable amount of traffic.

Prize drawings are always effective, provided the winners must be on the floor to obtain a ticket. It also helps to award prizes only to those in attendance at the drawing, but this is not always practical.

Associations use a variety of food services to increase floor traffic between meetings. If there is no large luncheon included with the price of registration, food should be served in the exhibit area that day. Some nonprofits have commercial vendors; others offer free sandwiches or snacks with soft drinks and beer.

Cocktail receptions with hors d'oeuvres are popular with attendees, but if not conducted properly they will produce few positive results. One or two large bars near the exhibit area entrance will only concentrate people in a single area. There is no incentive to examine the many exhibits. One means of alleviating the congestion is to locate bars in the far corners of the area, to encourage registrants to circulate. Another solution is to have waiters or waitresses walk throughout the area with trays of mixed and soft drinks. An experienced exhibit manager can actually control the flow of traffic by having the service help appear from side entrances with drinks, drawing attendees from the more congested areas. This approach is effective with thirsty patrons, but not with the wine and cheese crowd.

The final piece of the direct mail package is the order form. Ask exhibitors to list their first three booth preferences as they appear on the floor plan. To reserve the desired space, they must enclose a check. It may be for one-third or one-half the total cost, but the balance must be paid before they set up on the exhibit floor.

Since location is of primary importance to them, and space cannot be reserved without a down payment, checks should start to arrive shortly after the mailings are received. Postmarks determine priority when booth spaces are allocated.

Rules and regulations are usually spelled out on the back of the order form. This information is provided by the exhibit management firm or the hotel, when an exhibit area is managed by the nonprofit's staff.

For exhibitor mailings, cover letters are not mandatory; the materials speak for themselves. One exception would be the first time an organization decides to have exhibits. Then the executive director can explain the rationale in a cover letter and describe the organization, its purpose, and types of members who attend its meetings. Another exception would be local or state events where a brochure is not used, and the information is simply stapled together. Then it would be helpful to describe the event and location, with a personal invitation to exhibit. The letter need not be individually addressed; use a headline as a substitute for the salutation, but sign it at the bottom.

If the mailing consists only of a brochure and order form, be certain that both pieces stress the urgency of reserving space with a check by explaining that booths will be assigned according to the postmarks. Include with all mailings a self-addressed reply envelope to be certain the order form and check are mailed to the proper person.

The number of mailings to each list is optional. Targeted lists such as exhibitors at related conventions and associate members should receive at least three mailings. Advertisers in the organization's publications warrant two mailings, and potential associate members and advertisers should receive at least one.

After the first mailing, wait three weeks before making follow-up calls. By that time those exhibitors most interested will have reserved space.

Telephone Follow-up. In calling potential exhibitors, do take no for an answer. Unlike advertising sales, which are an ongoing process with repeated follow-up calls and letters, those in charge of exhibiting will usually express interest or the lack of it during the first call.

If interested, they will ask intelligent questions and may express their doubts or concerns. They may hesitate to send a check right away, or there may be questions about timing conflicts or projected attendance figures.

Answer all questions and attempt to obtain the order with one telephone call. If they are interested but hesitant, stay with them until a decision is made. If they are not interested and reject the offer, take their word for it and do not bother them with another follow-up call. Go back to them again next year.

As with membership sales, the primary reason for following direct mail with a call is to bring the mailing to the recipients' attention and press for a decision. If they do not remember seeing the packet but appear interested, send them another.

For those who have not discarded the mailing, ask if they are considering the offer to exhibit. Explain the high points of the meeting or convention, quality of attendees, added events on the exhibit floor, and the desire to do everything to make it a profitable occasion for exhibitors. In short, Sell.

Go first to those on the targeted lists. Call associate members who are major exhibitors at related conventions. Attempt to bring in companies that usually rent large three or four booth areas. Also attempt to sell a well-known company in each major product or service category.

Small exhibitors, those renting one or two booths, follow their leading competitors. If the major companies are not represented, they will have little interest in attending.

The large exhibitors also attract smaller companies trying to sell them products—subcontractors selling primes. Their sales reps can wander around the area in off times, getting to know representatives of the larger companies.

By concentrating on major exhibitors at the early stages of telephoning, exhibit salespeople are in a much better position to tout them to smaller companies during later calls.

After phoning those with exhibit budgets, call the organization's associate members who do not ordinarily exhibit. Many will exhibit just to support their nonprofit and its members, but it helps to be able to cite those companies that have already agreed to exhibit.

Advertisers in the association's publications are potential exhibitors, too, but the sale may be difficult. Having an advertising budget does not necessarily mean that they also have an exhibit budget.

When advertisers do exhibit, the decision is seldom made by the advertising department; sales or marketing managers must be contacted. Even though the advertising manager can supply their names, those who make the decisions to exhibit must also receive sales materials and follow-up calls.

If a nonprofit organization has a telemarketing operation, it can be extremely helpful in screening potential exhibitor lists for those who are interested. Telemarketers can be trained to sell exhibit space or turn over those with questions to an exhibit salesperson. When there are hundreds of associate members and advertisers to be called, telemarketing is a very efficient means of screening or selling.

In the final weeks before the convention, prospects are narrowed down to the foot draggers. Then it is desirable for the caller to be capable of assigning the remaining booths on the spot to close a sale.

It is understood, however, that a check must be mailed immediately to hold the desired exhibit space.

After exhibitors have been identified, informed, and sold, the real test begins—on the exhibit floor.

Exhibit Sales Retention

It is not unusual for nonprofits to ignore their exhibitors during the convention. They are frequently considered "vendors" who are a necessary but distracting adjunct not directly linked to the lofty agenda of the meetings. Nonprofit personnel, particularly those in nonmarketing roles, tend to cater to their more prominent members while exhibitors are ignored—left in an adjoining area to fend for themselves.

If their needs are not met, exhibitors will not return. Easily avoided minor irritants will cause them to grumble among themselves, causing defections that can siphon nondues revenue. To offset this, consider these exhibit retention strategies:

1. Hold a preconvention reception for exhibitors, in recognition of their support.
2. Conduct a meeting with exhibitors on opening day, outlining events and answering questions.
3. Have an association booth on the exhibit floor, manned by those in marketing positions.
4. Have a special area for exhibitors, where they can relax or become acquainted with one another.
5. Encourage floor traffic with announcements in the meeting rooms and special events.

A preconvention reception for exhibitors may seem extravagant, but when exhibit income is a significant portion of a nonprofit's total revenue, it is a gesture that demonstrates appreciation for their considerable support.

At major conventions, exhibits must be set up before opening day. Since association management and the board of directors also check in the day before, a reception that evening is a gracious means of bringing exhibitors together with the organization's leadership. Instead of a reception, smaller meetings and conventions might offer a continental breakfast for exhibitors on opening day. The cost is not prohibitive, but again it displays recognition, especially when management and department heads drop by. A few handshakes can make exhibitors feel they are an important part of the convention's success.

Before the floor is opened, there should be a meeting of exhibitors and those in the organization who are in charge of the convention. An association executive should welcome them and explain what has been planned to increase traffice in the exhibit area. The exhibit firm manager can go through the housekeeping rules, hours, and security concerns. Then the meeting should be opened to questions, and there will be many. This is the critical time to handle problems and complaints.

Another crucial damage control device is an association booth in a prominent location on the exhibit floor. It should be manned by those who work with associate members and advertisers, plus others involved in revenue-producing activities. An association booth pays for itself. Memberships, insurance, subscriptions, books, special reports, audiovisual materials, and promotional items are examples of products and services (that can be sold) to attendees and other exhibitors.

Added to the sales potential, though, is the opportunity for staff members to mingle with and listen to exhibitors. Membership people talk with current and potential associate members, and advertising people can strengthen their relationships with regular and prospective advertisers.

In addition, when exhibitors have problems, they can bring them directly to someone at the association's booth. There will be those with legitimate concerns and others who are chronic complainers. If left to themselves, those who are disgruntled will carry their grievances to other exhibitors.

While not practical at smaller conventions, a separate lounge or refreshment area for exhibitors is another convenience they will appreciate. After standing at a booth for several hours, exhibitors need an area where they can relax apart from attendees—a private place for selling each other or job shopping.

Nonprofit personnel on the exhibit floor should monitor the effectiveness of special events. Because they are preplanned, there is little control over planned attractions, but they can determine their value for the future. Do prize drawings bring large numbers of attendees to the exhibit area? Are the prizes appropriate or sufficiently valuable to produce a crowd? Do attendees leave immediately after the drawings or do they make the rounds while there? Are receptions well attended? Do people circulate?

After each event, talk with exhibitors throughout the area to gauge their reactions. Do they believe it was effective? If not, why not? This is walking remedial research—it is better to give them a chance to complain to their hosts than to each other.

Many problems will arise. There is seldom sufficient traffic to please those located farthest from the entrances, but just by being there to field complaints you may be able to smooth ruffled feathers. On the constructive side, you will learn much to improve the situation in the years ahead.

Hospitality Suites

Many exhibitors traditionally have hospitality suites in the convention hotel to provide comfortable quarters for their staff and as an adjunct to their exhibit sales efforts. They exhibit products and services on the floor, then invite favored and prospective customers to their suites for refreshments.

Until recently, most nonprofit organizations did not consider suites as revenue producers. Attendees and exhibitors arranged their own hotel accommodations, but this led to complications. Rather than pay the expense to exhibit, a few companies took over the suites and used them to conduct business with attendees. With no control over the suites, the association was deprived of any revenue from the mavericks.

To counter the situation, many nonprofits now negotiate with their convention hotels to take over all suite sales. The hotel will insist on reserving a few suites for its preferred guests, but generally will turn over control of the remaining suites to the association. The organization may retain a few suites for its own use, perhaps for the president or prominent guest speakers. All other suites are sold by the association along with exhibits. Those who rent hospitality suites must pay a surcharge in addition to the regular hotel suite rates.

The association maintains control and receives added income. As with exhibitors, suite sales are on a first-come, first-served basis. Those requesting suites list their first three preferences, and the reservations people allocate them as the checks and hotel registration forms arrive. Suite rental information is included in the direct mail packet to potential exhibitors. There are no separate mailings for this purpose.

Some nonprofit organizations impose strict conditions on hospitality suites. Although not required to be exhibitors, everyone residing in the convention suites must be fully registered for the convention. The organization also controls the hours and conditions to be observed. For example, one association requires that hospitality suites be closed while convention meetings are in session. There are strict limits on noise and suites are asked to be closed by 1:00 a.m. Every suite must be open to all registered attendees, although back rooms can be reserved for serious business discussions.

Analyzing the Results

As with membership and advertising sales, exhibit and suite rental results should be analyzed following each convention.

Were the exhibitors happy? What was the reaction of registrants to both exhibits and suites? How did sales compare with the previous year? What are sales projections for next year?

If membership, advertising, and exhibits people were on the floor during the convention, a follow-up study of exhibitors is unnecessary. Notes will have been taken on problems, complaints, and helpful suggestions. Observations of the special events and exhibitors' reactions will also be recorded for next year's planning. Registrants should receive a short follow-up questionnaire. Ask them to grade or comment on the various meetings, speakers, luncheons, and other events, but also determine how many visited the exhibit area, how much time was spent on the exhibit floor, and elicit their comments on exhibits and suites. Even though they are income producers, exhibits and suites should also be regarded favorably by members who attend the conventions.

How did exhibit and suite sales compare with the previous year? Can the differences be explained? Did the convention location affect floor attendance? Is the economy or state of the industry a factor?

Projecting next year's exhibit and suite sales calls for the same questions concerning location and the economy. Perhaps even more important is the mood of exhibitors as the convention closed. Were they satisfied with the attendance? Did they express concerns about next year's location or attendance?

Unsold exhibit space compares with unsold seats on an airline flight; they can never be sold at a later date. Sales projections are extremely important because they assist management in planning future conventions. Too much unsold space is costly and gives the appearance of less traffic; too little space reserved in advance means revenue lost.

Small nonprofit organizations need not look with envy at the enormous amount of income generated from exhibit and suite sales by many large trade associations. They can profit, too, if they have an annual meeting of their members. All groups with a common interest or concern are made up of people who are potential buyers of certain types of products. The rewards can be proportionately satisfying, even when scaled down.

10. Gift Shops and Promotional Catalogs

Nonprofit organizations have discovered another healthy source of revenue through gift shops and promotional catalogs. Museums, zoos, and other institutions open to the public have gift shops for their visitors. Associations frequently publish promotional catalogs filled with items that relate to the industry or professions of their members.

The Pacific Whale Foundation (PWF) crew on Maui hands out coupons to those leaving its whale watchers tours. The coupons offer free humpback whale notecards redeemable at the nearby Ocean Store. The store sells hats, T-shirts, sweatshirts, golf shirts, and tank shirts with whales and the PWF emblem. It also sells posters, books, and other gifts related to marine life.

The PWF magazine, *Fin & Fluke*, contains a gift catalog in the back of each issue picturing clothing, posters, coffee mugs, and bumper stickers. The order form includes a membership form and offers a 10 percent discount on all merchandise purchased by PWF members.

The Saint Louis Zoo and Chicago's Adler Planetarium have free admission to all visitors. The Zootique and the Adler Gift Shop, however, are income producers through the sale of a wide variety of gift items, books, and posters. The Zootique items are animal-related, while Adler sells globes, games, and books on astronomy.

Even though they charge admission to nonmember visitors, the Los Angeles County Museum of Art has a Museum Shop. It offers a 10 percent discount to members, as does the Saint Louis Zoo.

The National Association of Broadcasters (NAB) performs a beneficial promotional service for its radio and television station members. Stations can order from NAB a variety of promotional items customized to feature their call letters or logos for use as gifts to advertisers or to promote their stations.

The NAB Services Promotional Catalog includes the following items sold to members in quantity, *each with the member station's logo:*

- microphone flags (to identify the station)
- brass boxes, note-pad holders, pen stands, coasters, key holders, business card cases, letter openers, and calculator/cases
- station ID pins, lapel tacs, and key chains
- clocks and watches
- radios, license plate frames, and display plates
- coffee mugs, thermometers, calculators, pens, and markers

NAB also has a small gift shop in its Washington headquarters lobby with books, reports, clothing, and other broadcasting-related products, many featuring the NAB logo.

The Marine Corps Association (MCA) has a bookstore in its Quantico, Virginia, headquarters building featuring posters and military books, particularly by and about Marines. The store and the Bookservice Catalog also sell customized gift items with the USMC insignia.

The MCA not only sells books and Marine memorabilia to its members, it is also a major provider to other Marine Corps organizations. Marine Corps bases each have four or five annual balls for enlisted, senior enlisted, and officers, and they can order party supplies with the USMC insignia from the MCA, such as tablecloths, paper plates, plastic glasses, flag sets, placemats, balloons, cocktail napkins, stirrers, and coasters.

Items are promoted through stuffers enclosed in letters to new members as well as renewals. Anyone who calls for information is sent a free catalog, as are those who place orders.

These nonprofit organizations are careful to sell items related to their basic purpose, since income from unrelated trade or business activities is taxable. In addition, few of the items sold can be obtained at commercial retail outlets.

Store Operations

Managing a nonprofit store generally requires retailing experience. Seldom does an organization have qualified personnel who can take over a retail store, although there are notable exceptions.

Not even marketers of memberships, advertising, sales promotion, or exhibits have the background required for successful retailing. Consider what is expected of a good store manager:

- *Buying*—requires a thorough knowledge of prospective customers, including demographics, purchasing power, and buying habits. It also calls for negotiating with vendors, and knowing how much to buy.
- *Pricing*—what markups can be sustained for moving goods at a profit? Are there discounts for members? How are slow-moving items discounted without tarnishing the organization's image?
- *Displaying*—an art backed by a true understanding of the customers. Nonprofit stores require dignified displays, yet have the appeal to consummate on-the-spot sales.
- *Managing People*—the nonprofit manager must be able to hire and manage good sales personnel, many—including volunteers— without work experience. And store personnel must be trained to be polite and pleasant, with an understanding of the needs of the organization's members or visitors, as well as of the products sold. In retail, employee turnover can be a problem.

If store sales are stagnant or declining, it may be advisable to retain an outside retail consultant. When opening a store for the first time, look to the outside for someone with successful retail management experience. Managers can be very young, for department stores train assistant buyers and buyers who have just graduated from college; they can also be mature, with many years of experience. There are well-qualified people of all ages who would welcome escaping from the competitive, crisis-laden atmosphere of today's commercial retailing marketplace.

Catalog Operations

Nonprofit organizations with direct mail catalog operations require managers with other skills. When they also have a store, these capabilities are needed: (in addition to those just mentioned)

- *Advertising and Direct Mail Promotion.* Unless there is a separate marketing department, the manager should have the ability to work with photographers, printers, and writers in preparing ads and catalogs; know where to advertise, in addition to the organization's own publications; and be able to experiment with lists used for direct mail purposes.
- *Running a Fulfillment Operation.* Managers hire and direct part-time employees and/or volunteers to warehouse, package, invoice, and fulfill orders in a short turnaround period. Morale makes the difference, and managers are responsible for creating the desired environment.
- *Inventory Control.* While also essential in managing a store, inventory control is critical with direct mail orders. In addition to knowing how much to buy and when to reorder, it is important to know at all times what stock is available. Missent orders, damaged goods, and possible theft may escape the eyes of the computer's inventory records.

A nonprofit pondering the sale of promotional or gift items for the first time may ask the same question posed when considering the sale of advertising: "Is it worth it?"

Gift shops and promotional catalogs are definitely worthwhile when properly managed. They can contribute tremendously to the bottom line. When the products are of high quality, they add to an organization's stature, extending their value far beyond mere income production.

Associations also benefit their members and the industry or profession they serve. Promotional items of high quality serve to speak out with pride. Broadcasters are proud of their radio and television stations, and of being part of the broadcasting industry. Marines are proud to be Marines, and their pride in the Corps is demonstrated by Marine memorabilia years after separation from military service.

Gifts and promotional items directly related to the purpose of a nonprofit organization will please its members, enhance the image of the institution or association, and, when properly managed, make a generous financial contribution.

11. Negotiating Member Services

Membership organizations are constantly pursued by companies offering special discounts or services to members. Insurance companies, banks, long-distance carriers, car rental firms, and airlines besiege nonprofits with plans that will save members' money and increase nondues revenue.

They are looking for exclusive access to the organizations' mailing lists. Many will promise the moon, but it is management's responsibility to protect the interests of the organization and particularly its members.

Everything is negotiable. In negotiating, consider the members first, then the organization. How will the members benefit? Is the benefit real in terms of lower cost or improved service?

How will the organization benefit? Will an insurance or credit card plan provide cash benefits on top of member benefits? If a service is very advantageous to members, the nonprofit may receive little income for itself, but it should never lose money. Who will pay for the printing, mailing, advertising, and promotion?

The membership mailing list is the key to all negotiations. The larger or more valuable the list is to those offering financial and travel services, the more they are willing to give to the institution or association and its members. The actual lists should always be controlled by the nonprofit. If released, they could be duplicated and reused by any number of commercial enterprises. All mailings, though paid for by banks, insurance companies, car rental firms, or airlines, should remain under the close supervision of the nonprofit. Membership lists are the family jewels. If they are turned over there is nothing to negotiate.

Here are basic ingredients that determine the commercial value of a mailing list:

- Number of individual names and addresses
- Demographics
- Purchasing and travel habits
- Savings and investments

Service companies look for large numbers of up-to-date names of people who have a common interest or concern. Depending on the service offered, they may be interested in young people who are spending most of their disposable income, middle-aged savers looking toward retirement, or those over 65 concerned with supplementary health and long-term care plans. Associations with corporate members have a special appeal, for members with expense accounts travel and entertain far more than their personal incomes alone would permit.

Bank Credit Cards

Banks with MasterCard or Visa plans have a tendency to say, "You can make a million," on their initial interviews with nonprofit management. Under careful scrutiny, not only may the million be reduced to a few thousand dollars per year, but what do the members receive in return?

When meeting with a bank representative, ask these questions:

1. What annual percentage interest rate will be charged for member purchases?
2. What is the annual card fee to members?
3. How much will the nonprofit organization receive for each bank card issued to its members?
4. What percentage of members' annual card purchases will the organization receive?

Interest rates vary considerably. Nonprofit managers should be aware of prevailing rates charged the general public vs. prevailing discount rates available to membership organizations.

In the May 17, 1991, edition of the *Washington Post*, American Express ran a full-page advertisement to its cardholders, offering them a special discount if they sign up for the Optima Card. The regular American Express card charges are payable in 30 days, but the new Optima Card offers extended payment similar to MasterCard and Visa.

The headline read: "Why pay VISA or MasterCard over 19.00% a year—when you have a smarter option at 16.25%." According to the footnote, 19.0 percent is "based on the average of the 8 largest standard VISA/MasterCard issuers' APRs as published in the Main Survey of *RAM Research's Bankcard Update* 3/91."

If 19 percent is the average interest rate charged the general public, what discount is available to membership organizations? This is where the negotiating begins.

Many associations today subscribe to plans that charge members between 17 percent and 18 percent. Mercantile Bank, however, charges only 15.9 percent to Saint Louis Zoo Friends. That is a substantial member benefit.

Annual card rates are usually free the first year and $30 to $35 after that. UCLA alumni are charged a flat $20 per year by First Interstate Bank. After three years, their cardholders come out ahead. The UCLA Alumni also benefits. First Interstate gives the association a "donation" when UCLA members "obtain and use" the prestigious card featuring Royce Hall. Supplemental benefits should also be compared. Some banks insure against purchase losses, others have major lines of credit and quick processing of credit increase requests.

How do the nonprofit organizations benefit? Most banks are currently offering $1 for every new credit card issued to members. Even though as many as 10,000 members may take advantage of the offer, the organization would receive only $10,000.

Mercantile Bank gives the Saint Louis Zoo $5 per new cardholder. That results in $50,000 for every 10,000 new cardholders. And the bank pays for all printing and mailing costs, as do most plans.

The Saint Louis Zoo benefits more than $5 per cardholder. On the outside envelope to Zoo Friends the mailing quotes Zoo director, Charles Hoessle:

"Every purchase you make with the St. Louis Zoo Friends MasterCard will help support the Zoo's endangered species conservation efforts."

Mercantile Bank returns .25 percent of all purchases by its members to the zoo at the end of each year. This is not only unique—everyone is ahead. Zoo Friends receive a genuine discount, the zoo is compensated well, and the bank gains status as a supporter of one of the area's most beloved institutions.

When approached by a bank for credit card sponsorship, ask what percentage of purchases will be refunded to the nonprofit organization. In most cases, the million-dollar offer will dissipate. The question may be dismissed with a laugh as being naive, but pursue it. If the organization lends its name and its list to a bank, it deserves compensation beyond $1 per new card issued.

Persistent negotiations frequently produce another offer, though vague. Banks may promise a certain percentage of purchases after a test period, but the nonprofit is expected to rely entirely on the bank's accounting methods. Pin them down. An independent audit or spot-check of members' annual purchases should be verified. Before signing an agreement, know and be able to confirm specific benefits to members and to the organization. It may be fashionable to offer members a credit card with the nonprofit's name and logo, but it is not always profitable. If the bank's final offer is skimpy, reject it. There are many other banks.

Insurance Plans

It is difficult, if not impossible, to compare insurance plans of one nonprofit organization with those of another.

With insurance, *absolutely everything is negotiable.* Instead of merely comparing a proposed plan with those of other nonprofits, ask several carriers to come in and make point-by-point comparisons.

One unnamed association has just gone through this process. After prolonged negotiations, a formal agreement, and a four-year test period followed by recent negotiations with other underwriters and administrators, the association is comfortable with this arrangement:

1. The *Administrator* receives:
   - 11 percent of the annual premiums paid by members as an administrative fee,
   - free advertising in association publications, and
   - direct mail printing, reimbursable at cost.
2. The *Association* receives:
   - 3 percent of the annual premiums,
   - one-third of the surplus of premiums paid after claims at the end of each three-year period, and
   - free mailings.
3. The *Underwriter* receives:
   - 86 percent of the annual premiums and
   - two-thirds of the surplus of premiums after claims.

Many administrators charge considerably more than 11 percent, and their fees may not be negotiable. Underwriters faced with more claims than premiums can back out of an agreement. In some cases, the nonprofit organization may be faced with a penalty when there is no surplus after a three-year period.

Again, negotiating calls for a delicate balance of satisfying the interests of members, the organization, the administrator, and the underwriter. If any of the four are at the short end, renegotiating resumes.

The insurance industry, with its actuarial and risk tables, can take care of itself. Administrators and underwriters are not going to lose money over an extended period. If they are not complaining, however, there could be excessive profits at the expense of the association and its members.

With financial services, negotiation is a top management function, not a marketing function. In some cases, marketing management may be entrusted to negotiate telephone and travel discounts, but bank credit cards and insurance have a direct effect on the well-being of members and their families.

Long-distance Cards

Very little hard negotiating is possible with the long-distance carriers, since there are only three—AT&T, MCI, and U.S. Sprint. They are extremely competitive, though, so the nonprofit may extract a few concessions in return for lending its name to a carrier.

Consider the member discount proposals of all three. A typical U.S. Sprint offer is:

- 10 percent off daytime calls
- 4 percent off evening calls
- 3 percent off night and weekend calls
- 5 percent off Dial 1 WATS daytime interstate calls

While traveling, members can use the FONCARD and be eligible for the discounts. Members who are already U.S. Sprint customers can receive these discounts on their business or personal phones with no hassle. Those who are currently AT&T or MCI customers, however, must sign an authorization form to have their local telephone companies switch carriers to U.S. Sprint, which may require a service fee.

Since there is a possibility of confused and disgruntled members, the discounts should be worthwhile to members. And the organization, too, should receive more than free stuffers for its member mailings. After determining member discounts, ask the long-distance carrier representative these questions:

1. How much are you willing to pay the organization for each member who converts from another service to your service?
2. Are you willing to refund a small percentage of the long-distance revenue received from our members?
3. Would your company consider cosponsoring any of our special events or participating in any of our fund-raising projects?
4. Will you back up the affiliation by advertising in our newsletter, magazine, or directory?
5. Will you provide promotional materials and special mailings if we agree to include your brochure in selected mailings to our members?

It is impossible to know how many companies and nonprofits are paid for revenue produced by their customers or members. Airlines, for example, must conduct heavy negotiating with long-distance telephone carriers in return for their frequent fliers' lists.

When a nonprofit has a valuable list of frequent travelers or those in a position to change carriers for their business phones, it, too, should negotiate a fee per card and percentage of long distance revenue. Associations with members who make the average number of long-distance calls have nothing to lose by asking for card and revenue fees or "donations." If they are turned down, they can pursue the next step by negotiating for paid advertising support through their association publications. Health, educational, and cultural institutions may negotiate for sponsorships or donations. Their members or donors are very often high-income families whose actions can influence others.

It may sound distasteful, but there is no reason to undervalue membership lists. Commercial companies know that affiliations with nonprofit organizations can be extremely profitable. As long as agreements are open and benefit the organization (and not individuals within the organization), they cannot be construed as anything but legitimate.

Car Rental Cards

Car rental companies do not issue credit cards; they issue discount cards. Similar to the long-distance carriers, they want to be affiliated with nonprofits so that their members will carry the discount cards in wallets and purses along with credit cards. The company hopes that when members rent cars, they will select the company that offers a discount.

The typical member benefit is 10 percent off the going rates, and occasionally an upgrade. The nonprofit organization receives very little, if anything, in return for the use of its mailing list. Some companies will offer considerably more, but check out their reputations and ability to meet the needs of the membership. How many airports do they service? Are they located in the airports, or in outlying areas? Do they have new cars, and are they clean?

Negotiating with reputable national firms is difficult, but worth the effort. If the institution or association has publications that accept advertising, attempt to reach an agreement on a specific number of advertising pages to be placed each year in return for issuing a car rental discount card to new members.

When there is no potential advertising to negotiate, discuss cosponsorships of special events or an exchange of free rented cars for the issuance of discount cards. For example, an association with a monthly magazine might agree to send a car rental firm's card to all its members if it will pay for three or four pages of advertising per year. A hospital might issue the card to its donors if the firm loans cars for its annual golf tournament. There, too, the car rental firm would have high visibility and recognition for its "donation."

It is advisable to press for at least a three-year agreement. The major rental companies keep meticulous records on computer. If they are not satisfied with the volume of rentals per year by an organization's members, they will balk at investing additional dollars in advertising or providing "services in kind." If that occurs, negotiate with other car rental companies. Take the best offer back to the firm that is attempting to renege on its agreement. Unless it is willing to at least match the best offer, change affiliations.

When a satisfactory agreement cannot be reached with a single firm, some associations work with more than one. The competition broadens the discount possibilities for members, but dilutes the annual rental volume for the car rental companies.

In the long run, the membership department benefits most from car rental discount cards. They add to the list of membership benefits, and members do appreciate receiving discount cards in their new member packages, whether they use them or not.

Travel Services

Airlines, hotels, and travel agencies will also negotiate with nonprofit organizations in order to provide their services. Convention planners negotiate with airlines that serve the convention city for the best discounts, and with convention hotels for registration discounts and free rooms and suites to accommodate its staff.

Airlines have only seats to offer, but hotels have far more than rooms. Depending on the size of the convention, a hotel may agree to provide free meeting space, donate coffee breaks, or even sponsor a reception. Negotiating with hotels requires years of experience, and details must be covered in writing. With large conventions, association management, convention management, and the organization's attorney should all be involved.

Nonprofits that do not have conventions frequently offer tours and cruises for their members. This requires the selection of a reliable travel agent. Discounts are important, but the organization and quality of tours are paramount. Anything that can happen will. Members and reliable donors can be soured on an organization that sponsors poorly run tours or cruises. Charter flights should leave their destinations on time. The choice of hotels, bus lines, and cruise lines can make a vacation memorable or miserable. Care must be taken that members are not exploited, not taken from one tourist trap to another. Free time should be available. Food should be of good quality and meals should be served on time. Medical facilities with good doctors should be readily available. Painstaking details must be worked out with the travel agent well in advance.

With the exception of hotels, nonprofits have little to gain from tours and cruises other than the goodwill of their members. They can, however, do everything possible to break even, at the very least. Brochures and other travel literature should be provided at no cost to the organization. When possible, airlines, hotels, and travel agents should be encouraged to advertise in the sponsoring organization's publications, even given an advertising discount.

Members expect their nonprofit organizations to provide them with solid information as part of their dues. Newsletters, magazines, letters from the president address their common interests and concerns. They also expect fiscal responsibility. Members may appreciate other benefits including insurance, credit cards, and travel discounts but they should understand that at no time should expenses exceed income for the sake of a fringe benefit.

12. Fund Raising

How do most nonprofit organizations originate? How do they expand when new construction projects are necessary? How do they meet impending legislative or regulatory threats? What can they do to supplement membership and nondues income? Fund raising.

Community institutions such as museums, hospitals, symphonies, zoos, and colleges are founded with donations that are sometimes matched by local tax dollars. An individual with a large art collection may set up a trust fund to establish a local museum. Religious organizations may sponsor new hospitals or colleges. A group of local corporate donors may decide the community should have a symphony, theater, aquarium, planetarium, or zoo.

Associations are usually formed by major corporations within an industry. When smaller companies feel that attention is not being paid to their particular needs, they may organize a splinter group and form their own association. The same is true of the professions, including legal, medical, real estate, accounting, and the military, among others.

Public interest groups may originate with smaller-scale donors, but it still requires seed money to incorporate as a nonprofit organization before memberships can be offered.

After they are established, most nonprofits sell memberships to finance their organizations. Adding large numbers of members brings more community involvement in local institutions, and adds political clout to associations and public interest groups.

Members expect a newsletter or magazine for their dues, but they also look for increased benefits. Most of these benefits add to an organization's nondues income. Members and suppliers are willing to purchase directories, special reports, books, cassettes, advertising, exhibit space, and promotional items. The combination of membership dues and nondues income sustains nonprofits during ordinary times.

Hospitals, however, do not have ordinary memberships to sell. Patients are not required to join before being admitted. Universities have alumni groups, but without large donors and other fund-raising activities, they would suffer.

When public and private nonprofits need to expand or renovate, they have no choice but to turn to fund raising for their capital projects. Even though they may have both dues and nondues income, fund-raising projects will make the difference in meeting construction goals. Associations and professional societies occasionally buy or build headquarters buildings, but normally their fund-raising requirements are far more urgent.

Their reserves are seldom sufficient to cover threatening legislative or regulatory proposals which might damage the industry or profession they represent. Lobbying efforts are costly, and must be conducted in a short period of time. That means raising additional cash or pledges from members and, sometimes, nonmembers.

Fund-raising Techniques

Nonprofit fund-raising techniques are varied; each day enterprising people envision innovative methods to fund their organizations. Potential major donors are called on in person, visited by someone they respect, someone who can appeal to them on a peer level. While individual donors may agree with the fund raiser's purpose, they may in turn seek ego gratification, tax advantages, or estate protection. Corporate donors must be shown that their contributions can enhance the reputation of the company within the community or help protect the interests of their industry.

The use of citywide special events is another widely employed fund-raising technique. Marathons, golf tournaments, phonathons, balls, municipal picnics, and parades are very successful when properly organized.

Nonprofits often develop suborganizations, support groups that use social gatherings for charitable causes. People with the same social backgrounds or interests sponsor parties, balls, or auctions to benefit their favorite charities.

On a smaller scale, nonprofit institutions may appeal to families or elementary school students to assist them through adoption programs, financed with lunch money contributions or recycling programs.

Understanding the Donor

Donors vary in their ability to contribute, and in their vantage points. Wealthy contributors are not motivated by direct mail. Many shun publicity, and prefer to be called on by appointment in their homes. They are asset preservationists.

High-income (but not necessarily wealthy) donor prospects have their own agenda. Most are attempting to build, rather than preserve, an estate. They can be approached through appropriate direct mail appeals, but usually require telephone follow-ups.

Corporate donors are sympathetic toward improving their community and its institutions. They also expect recognition for their companies and top executives.

Support groups consist of the socially active. With higher-than-average incomes, they like to mingle with their peers. As they climb social and corporate ladders, members of support groups and their spouses understand what can be accomplished by supporting worthy causes.

Special events appeal to the community at large, across the social and financial spectrum. Publicity and advertising swell attendance, and all involved are pleased to participate.

Lobbying support is not philanthropic. Legislative or regulatory intrusions on an industry or profession can result in a drastic drop in profits for businesses and professionals. Companies will give, but they do appreciate recognition and expect to be kept informed.

Individual Donors. In the late 1930s, the Archdiocese of Los Angeles asked the Sisters of Charity of Leavenworth, Kansas, to found a Catholic hospital on the west side of Los Angeles.

Four sisters arrived in Santa Monica, where they purchased five acres one mile from the ocean at a cost of $13,500. Through years of hard work and the help of the community, Saint John's Hospital opened in October 1942.

Today, 15 Sisters of Charity are assisted by nearly 2,000 employees, more than 1,000 physicians in 88 different medical specialties, and 300 active volunteers.

Saint John's current fund-raising campaign with a goal of $25 million, is titled "Our Commitment to Tomorrow." The hospital plans to raise $10 million for Saint John's Heart Institute, $7.4 million for technology and facilities, $5 million for Saint John's Cancer Center, and $2.6 million for the Saint John's Child Study Center, where "no child is turned away."

Major gifts from individual donors are essential since it is believed that $10 million will come from 20 to 30 people.

The Fund Development Campaign cannot rely on direct mail to potential contributors. For personal visits, the staff have prepared a 24-page, four-color brochure on coated stock with a complete description of Saint John's Hospital and Health Care Center, its accomplishments and goals.

Inside the back cover are individual sheets with dollar breakdowns of construction and equipment required for each center and a list of the foundation trustees, pillars of the Los Angeles social and business community. (Ronald Reagan is the honorary chairman.) Also included is a pledge card enabling the donor to enclose payment, pledge stock, be billed quarterly or annually, or agree to make a "Planned Gift." Donors designate how their gifts will be spent. It is noted, of course, that all donations are tax-deductible. A reply envelope is also enclosed.

Instead of being mailed, this all-inclusive brochure, titled "Our Commitment to Tomorrow," is left behind with prospective donors who cannot make an immediate decision.

Saint John's believes that "people give to people." It is essential that the "right" person meet with a prospective donor, for personal respect and mutual admiration are necessary for a successful call, according to the development staff.

The volunteer leader, known to the donor, takes the initiative in arranging the appointment and assumes the dominant role, accompanied by a staff support person. This support person may be the president of Saint John's, the executive vice president-development, one of the founders, or a renowned cancer or heart specialist, depending on the situation.

Before the visit, "proper and definitive research" is undertaken on the prospective donor. A target goal is also agreed on, and it is not a modest one. The volunteer is carefully schooled to understand the institution, to believe in the importance of major donations, and to be able to answer questions, such as the following:

- What is unique about Saint John's?
- Why is finishing the heart and cancer centers a vital undertaking?
- What difference will a major gift make?
- What will it mean to the community if a part of the Child Study Center is endowed?
- Why is it crucial that Saint John's be at the forefront in research technology and new equipment?

Volunteer preparation is critical. The caller must be convinced and excited regarding Saint John's future and its ability to deliver. Belief is contagious. One who knows the mission can share the dreams of Saint John's with prospective donors.

Volunteers are instructed to base their personal visits on these principles:

1. People will give when asked.
2. Donors give emotionally and spontaneously.
3. It is important to be a listener and allow the prospect to take the lead.
4. Ask for the gift; that is the reason for the call.
5. Be positive and joyful.
6. Donor recognition is important when soliciting gifts.

Though a donor decision is not expected on the first visit, callers are told the "moment of truth"—when a specific amount is asked for—should not linger. The staff person can assist them at this point.

When a decision is hanging at the conclusion of a meeting, the brochure is left behind for consideration. Discreet telephone calls and additional visits follow until a decision is made.

The potential donors discussed above are the select group of individuals who are truly "wealthy." Saint John's also has an annual giving campaign for individuals with high incomes. The principle here is expressed very clearly: "If you benefit the person, you will benefit the institution. If you begin with the institution's needs, you will lose the donor." That maxim could be applied to any marketing venture.

This annual giving campaign combines direct mail with telephone follow-ups. A simple two-color, four-panel brochure tells the story with its bold heads:

Cover: Has the IRS become your favorite charity?

Inside Panels: Now charity can turn tax money into retirement money.

The brochure describes the Saint John's Hospital Charitable Gift Annuity. Like a regular annuity, it provides fixed income for life. The difference is that a portion of the purchase price is tax-deductible, and when the annuity payments begin (usually at retirement), a portion of these payments is tax-free as well.

While Keoghs, IRAs, and pension and profit-sharing plans are good, they have their conditions and limitations. The brochure explains that the charitable gift annuity's only limitation is very liberal—up to half an individual's annual income.

It is "More than a Charity. A Good Investment," the brochure declares. A 40-year-old who invests $250,000 over a 25-year period (or $10,000 per year), will have $188,400 in tax deductions, with estimated tax savings of $65,375. At age 65, the annual annuity income will be nearly $34,000, with more than $3,000 of that tax-free.

After telling prospective investors they can designate how Saint

John's spends their money, it asks to meet with the individuals and their tax advisors:

> We'd like to explain all the advantages and benefits available, including joint survivorship, reduced taxes on your Social Security benefits, purchasing with property instead of cash, and much more.

And it concludes with the suggestion that the prospective donor call the hospital's director of planned giving.

Saint John's also has a separate campaign—more modest in scope—for physicians on its medical staff. Instead of seeking $10,000 per year, the Doctors Campaign suggests individual physicians pledge $10,000 over four years—$400 down and $200 per month for 48 months. This is not an annuity; it is a donation. This appeal is aimed more toward vanity or ego than to save on taxes, although donations are deductible.

The accompanying brochure is a glossy rich maroon with gold lettering on the cover, red on white inside, and reverse white on maroon on the back.

Under the heading, "For Physicians Only," the brochure explains the $25-million development program being launched by Saint John's.

Under the subhead, "What You Receive" it describes the following:

> . . . your name will be added to a new, elegantly-designed [sic] commemorative wall in the main lobby of the hospital . . . opposite . . . the wall which bears the names of our Board of Trustee members.
>
> In addition, you will receive a plaque for your office and a pin that identifies you as a contributor to the Doctors Campaign.
>
> Along with other members of the medical staff who have joined the program, you will participate in the decision of how and where the donated money will be used. Whenever donations are used to buy specific pieces of equipment or in facility renovation, a special plaque will identify the equipment or facility as having been donated by the physicians who participated in the Doctors Campaign.

It also points out a very practical reason for contributing:

By helping Saint John's to provide the leading advances in health care, you can continue to refer your patients there confident that state-of-the-art technology is available. As a physician, you will continue to benefit from high quality surgical, diagnostic, and treatment facilities purchased by generous donors like yourself.

The brochure urges its medical staff to become pacesetters by inspiring others to give. "It is the first step in making a commitment to a great tomorrow," the brochure concludes, "for yourself and for the institution in which you practice medicine."

For those unable to pledge $200 per month over four years, it asks for a pledge of a lesser amount each month, or a one-time gift. "However," it warns, "only those physicians making a $10,000 contribution will be included on the Honor Roll wall . . ."

This is an extremely effective direct mail piece. A flap inside the back cover contains a postage-paid reply pledge envelope that enables the individual physician to return a check for $400 or charge the donation to a bank credit card.

Individual donors, large and small, are given recognition in *St. John's News*, an attractive glossy tabloid with wide distribution. While names of donors are listed under their designated areas of giving, such as cancer research, the amounts are not mentioned.

Corporate Donors. Behind most successful community fund-raising activities are local business executives and their companies. In addition to financial donations, they provide sound management and assistance to the committees formed to raise money. Corporations sponsor events, they provide gifts-in-kind and services, and they match funds to involve their own employees in community charitable causes.

The Adler Planetarium conducted a capital improvement, "Campaign for Chicago's Brightest Star." Between October 1986 and January 1991 the capital campaign raised $7.1 million from corporations and individuals, surpassing its original goal of $6.5 million.

No direct mail was used—just personal fund-raising. Of the 15 donors of $100,000 or more, most were family trusts, foundations, or wealthy individuals. There was only one corporation and three corporate foundations.

Those giving $25,000 to $100,000, however, were primarily corporate donors or their foundations. Only four of the 21 were individuals. The 24 donors of $10,000 to $25,000 were almost evenly divided—13 corporate and 11 individuals.

On March 1, 1991 contributors to the capital campaign were invited to the ribbon-cutting for the new "Stairway to the Stars" escalator project. The escalator carried them from the Universe Theater directly into the Sky Theater surrounded by thousands of twinkling stars and galaxies. In the past, attendees had to trudge up three flights of stairs during the two-part Sky Show.

On the following night, March 2, all Adler Planetarium members were invited to a grand opening party to witness the Sky Show and the new escalator—the principle reason for the capital campaign.

The Saint Louis Zoo launched its first capital campaign in 1984 to build "The Living World," a facility that features the greatest variety of animal species and high-tech interpretive exhibits ever assembled. By 1989 the drive concluded with a total of $17.9 million raised, and the facility has since been built. Sixteen of the 20 largest donors ($100,000 or more) were corporations or corporate trusts, as were half of those donating $25,000 or more.

The Zoofair fundraiser was sponsored by 21 local corporations, one personal foundation, and 58 St. Louis-area restaurants. More than 1,500 guests dined and danced on the zoo grounds, enabling the zoo to raise $300,000 for its Endangered Species Research Center and Veterinary Hospital.

Since there are 58 corporations in the St. Louis area that provide matching gift funds to the zoo, many of these companies' employees are also motivated to become individual donors.

Companies offer the services of their management to attend and chair committee meetings, and many provide services and gifts-in-kind—bottlers provide beverages, car dealers provide transportation, and restaurants provide food, to name a few.

Special Events

Saint John's Hospital is a great believer in special events. Every other year they hold a Crystal Ball, for which everything is donated, including the dinner, the events, and the talent. At the 1990 Crystal

Ball, featuring Frank Sinatra, Saint John's raised $1 million at $25,000 per table.

Another annual event is a movie premier, the goal of which is to raise $500,000 through ticket sales. An anonymous donor supplements the balance, should the hospital fall short of its goal.

And then there is the Annual Jimmy Stewart Relay Marathon, an areawide extravaganza with something to offer all ages and incomes. It is free to the 30,000 spectators, but everyone else contributes, including the 5,000 runners, who are sponsored.

The marathon, cohosted by Jimmy Stewart and Robert Wagner, raises nearly $500,000 for the Saint John's Child Study Center.

Billed as "the largest relay marathon in the nation," the event consists of five-member teams with each member running a 5.2-mile loop through Los Angeles's Griffith Park. Spectators picnicking in the park can see each change of relays.

There are approximately 5,000 runners, or 1,000 relay teams. Instead of competing with each other, they compete in more than 25 categories such as "Entertainment," "Financial," "Mended Hearts," and "Golden Seniors." In past years the oldest runner was 83.

In the picnic area is a stage with constant entertainment during the marathon. A fire-eating unicyclist, bands, tap dancers, accordion players, and even a talent show by Saint John's employees add to the festivities and provide a focal point for a televised show of the annual event. All of the entertainment is donated.

Adjacent to the main stage area, companies exhibit or sell products from 10-ft. × 10-ft. booths equipped with a canopy, table, and chairs. Cost of the canopy and space is $1,000, although major corporate sponsors receive complimentary space.

The real money is raised through the sale of corporate sponsorships, at $500 per team. Nonprofits can sponsor a team for $125; the balance is made up by corporate sponsors.

During the 1991 10th annual Saint John's Relay Marathon, Jimmy Stewart appears on everything—posters, brochures, souvenir T-shirts, runners' T-shirts, volunteer's T-shirts, and newspaper advertising. Even the cocktail reception kickoff for large donors, where they can meet Stewart and Wagner, features Jimmy Stewart's likeness on the invitation.

The brochure sent to prospective corporate sponsors is particularly appealing. This four-color ten-panel piece describes the marathon and the benefits to donors and to Saint John's, and is highlighted with an abundance of white space and attractive snapshots of runners and celebrities.

Benefits to corporate sponsors, in addition to joining more than 200 other companies, include:

- Exposure to thousands of racers and spectators through banners, T-shirts, and other signage
- Publicity through numerous vehicles—the Jimmy Stewart Relay Marathon has appeared on numerous television entertainment and news programs and in countless other media outlets
- Builds team spirit and camaraderie among employees
- Develops community relations by showing that the company cares and is doing something for the children of southern California
- Provides a chance to be part of an exciting and popular event

Companies that cannot field a team of runners are encouraged to sponsor nonprofit teams such as firefighters, policemen, or students so they can participate in the marathon.

Two panels of the brochure list the corporate sponsors from the previous year's marathon. The back panel contains the pledge form for team sponsors or those companies simply willing to contribute a tax-deductible donation to the Saint John's Child Study Center. Companies with questions can ask to be called or be shown a six-minute video.

Why is this special event so effective? It has a special staff from Saint John's working full time, with a committee of 35 community leaders and company CEOs who volunteer their time and efforts to make it work. An avalanche of well-planned publicity, advertising, and direct mail, combined with two-person teams (volunteers and staff members) calling on major sponsors, results in raising nearly $500,000 for the Saint John's Child Study Center.

Few nonprofit institutions have the ability to bring together this combination of celebrities, executive muscle, and money, but special events are a successful fund-raising technique for nonprofit organizations all over the country.

Support Groups

Women outside of business are also active supporters of nonprofit organizations. Saint John's, for example, has a Hope Guild and the Irene Dunne Guild, the newest support group for the hospital.

The Hope Guild sponsors smaller social events, such as benefit balls and a day at the races. The Irene Dunne Guild recently completed fund raising for installation of VCRs in one wing of the hospital, and plans to install VCRs in all the patient rooms. Its spring fund raiser for the Saint John's Cancer Center sold $125 tickets to a private screening of a newly released movie, with a cocktail buffet, at the new I. M. Pei–designed Creative Artists Agency building.

These indefatigable volunteers can and do help to fund health, education, culture, and the arts in cities of every size. Symphonies, theaters, and museums would be strapped without their efforts, which focus on social functions and events. Most of these charitable efforts rely on very little staff assistance from their nonprofit beneficiaries.

Mundane chores are combined with social expertise. Talents include development of mailing lists, addressing, stuffing and mailing invitations, working with caterers and florists, decorating ballrooms and tables, hiring entertainment, making seating arrangements, and managing large sums of money.

Those in nonprofit organizations and the business world (the nine-to-fivers) may look with disdain at women's charitable organizations or support groups, but few could match their array of talent, energy, and single-minded dedication to worthy causes.

Family-oriented Programs

Many nonprofits are including families and school children as an important part of their fund-raising activities. Individual contributions are small, but the total amount raised is frequently substantial.

Soundings, the Pacific Whale Foundation's (PWF) Adopt-A-Whale newsletter, is mailed to schools and members twice a year. Those classrooms or schoolchildren who have adopted whales learn just where their "adoptees" have been sighted in the past six months.

Each adopted whale is listed by name, parents, date and location of sighting, and type of activity, such as swimming with other adults, with calf, or swimming alone, singing. By referring to a map of the islands in *Soundings*, the exact location can be determined. There are also photographs and names of whales that have not yet been adopted. The adoption fee for an unnamed exclusive whale is $75, and the annual support fee $50. The donor can name and personally adopt the whale. Prenamed nonexclusive whales can be adopted for only $15 annually.

Parents and grandparents may contribute the adoption fees to PWF, but many classrooms raise their own money with recycling programs in the schools. While only $30,000 is involved, the money does aid the PWF whale research and education programs.

In contrast, more than 9,000 St. Louis Zoo Parents members contribute well over $200,000 each year to the care and feeding of zoo animals. A mailing is sent to regular members (Zoo Friends) asking each family to adopt an animal of their choice for $25 to help provide for its nutritional needs.

The covering letter lists other benefits of Zoo Parenthood:

- A personalized Certificate of Adoption suitable for framing
- Parent's name listed on the Zoo Parent Kiosk at the South Entrance of the Zoo
- An attractive iron on T-shirt decal of the Parents Program logo
- An invitation to the annual behind-the-scenes picnic planned exclusively for Zoo Parents and their families.

Parenthood is also promoted as a gift:

Consider the gift of Zoo Parenthood! Even the person who has everything doesn't have a Siberian Tiger! Zoo Parent adoptions make unique gifts . . . that keep on giving . . . and living!

The enrollment form has an open amount for contributions, which can be paid by check or credit card. In addition, Zoo Parents is eligible for corporate matching gifts.

Looking to future donors, the zoo also has a club for young children, Zoo-MMM, with many corporate-sponsored educational and entertainment events, including the Zoolympics.

From grave to cradle, there are fund-raising plans that work well for nonprofits. Estate preservation, estate planning, tax savings plans, corporate and professional reputation enhancement, social functions, gala events, and adoption programs all appeal to certain ages and incomes—from the oldest and wealthiest citizens and corporations to young children who also learn the gift of giving.

13. Nondues Revenue Focus

Health, educational, cultural, and art institutions, associations, and public interest groups have a wide variety of nondues revenue-producing activities.

They may sell informational products, magazines, books, videos, computer software. Associations sell advertising, convention registrations, and exhibit space. Nonprofits derive additional income from gift shops or the sale of promotional items, insurance, and bank credit cards. Many engage in fund raising for capital expansion, acquisitions, or lobbying efforts.

Can a single nondues revenue marketing plan encompass all these activities? It depends on the organization structure, the mindset of the management, and its board of directors.

Each marketing activity must be funded, and that calls for budgets. When proposed budgets are based on sound marketing plans, they can be adjusted to meet management objectives, considering the money available and the dollar potential.

When budgets have been approved, who coordinates the marketing activities, dues and nondues income, including fund raising?

IV. COORDINATING MARKETING ACTIVITIES

Every nonprofit organization has a purpose. It may serve the health, educational, or cultural needs of the community. It may be a public interest group concerned with public policy or an association promoting and protecting the interests of an industry or profession.

More than 90 percent of nonprofit employees are engaged in fulfilling the original purpose of the organization. A university or hospital may have a development department for fund raising, but most of its staff comprises faculty educating students, or doctors, nurses, and attendants serving their patients.

This is also true of associations. Their membership departments, advertising, registration, and exhibits sales personnel constitute only a small part of the total staff. Attorneys, economists, researchers, editors, and librarians are there to serve the basic purpose of the association to promote and protect the interests of its members.

Today, marketing activities are essential for survival and growth, but where do they fit in? How can profit-oriented minds operate successfully without upsetting the nonprofit environment? It depends entirely on the CEO.

14. Importance of the CEO

The nonprofit chief executive determines the function, scope, and organization of income-producing activities. It is not imperative for the CEO to genuinely like marketing, only to understand it. Marketing is not simply a euphemism for "selling."

The marketing function as applied to any income-producing activity consists of:

- market research
- planning and budgeting
- promotion and advertising
- sales
- analysis

While promotion, advertising, and sales produce the income, they must be preceded by careful research, planning, and budgeting—then followed with objective analysis which will provide assistance in the next year's planning.

If the CEO believes marketing is merely "selling," marketing activities will be relegated to a lowly position in the nonprofit organization structure. Without benefit of high-level support, substantive research, and planning, most marketing activities will be doomed or remain stagnant.

When the CEO understands and appreciates the need for applying the marketing approach to income-producing activities, marketing will be given more prominence within the organization.

Prominence does not guarantee acceptance, however. For example, membership directors who conduct sporadic mailings, routinely maintain the membership lists, and mail renewal letters may resent the special training required in the techniques of market research, direct mail, and telephone follow-ups.

Marketing professionals brought in from the outside can expect varying degrees of hostility, aversion, nonacceptance, or amusement from staff members conditioned to a nonprofit environment. Good marketers, however, are people-oriented as well as profit-oriented. They can identify their activities with the common goals of the organization. For example:

- A fund raiser does not think like a hospital administrator or museum curator, but shares the goal of a new building or wing.
- An advertising salesperson does not think like an editor, but both want to improve the product with increased editorial pages, the use of color, better writing and graphics.
- A membership director does not think like a lobbyist, but both realize increased membership will result in more financial and political clout for the association.

It is the CEO's responsibility to make it understood throughout the organization that marketing is to be accepted as another essential element of good management. The marketing concept cannot be imposed with a single memorandum or a meeting of department heads; it is built into the budgeting process from the top down.

The chief executive also decides how the marketing functions are to be coordinated and administered. There are "inside" and "outside" executives. Both types can be highly successful, with proper backup.

"Outside" CEOs are spokespersons for the institutions or industries they represent. They travel, deliver speeches, testify before political bodies, and are frequently skilled fund raisers for their nonprofit organizations. They are high-profile executives. More often than not, "outside" CEOs came up through the ranks in their industry or profession. Universities may be headed by renowned educators, museums by curators, hospitals by physicians, zoos by zoologists, planetariums by astronomers, and trade associations by successful professionals or executives in their fields of interest. When they speak, "outside" CEOs speak with authority. They are respected by their peers and the community at large.

But who keeps the store? Nonprofit organizations have day-to-day activities that require management attention. The number two person may be a capable administrator who, regardless of title, acts as the chief operating officer (COO) and to whom departmental heads report. Another alternative may be an organization with strong department heads who report directly to the CEO. A third arrangement, particularly in very large organizations, is a strong group of department heads reporting to the COO.

In smaller organizations headed by "outside" executives, marketing activities are managed by a marketing coordinator who reports to the administrator, or by a marketing director who reports to the CEO. In larger nonprofits, the marketing coordinator or director usually reports to the chief administrator.

The worst-case scenario has down-the-line marketing people reporting only to their department heads, with no marketing coordinator or marketing director.

Nonprofit organization boards of directors are not always enamored of high-profile "outside" executives. Instead, they appoint the best administrators they can find to run their institutions or associations.

"Inside" CEOs are "hands-on" executives. Rather than spending much of their time making public appearances, they use prominent board or staff members to act as their spokespersons. They are in complete control of their organizations. "Inside" CEOs are administrators. They may be health administrators, education administrators, or business administrators, but they have come up through administrative management rather than through the industry or profession of the organizations they represent.

The number two person in the organization may be in the process of being groomed to take over when the CEO retires, or may be an administrative assistant who acts as an operations coordinator. Department heads, however, usually report directly to the "inside" CEO.

Authority may be delegated to department heads if the organization can afford to employ a high-quality staff of middle-management executives. The "inside" administrative CEO, however, controls the budgeting process of all departments regardless of the caliber of middle management.

Marketing activities can be assigned to a special assistant to the CEO who acts as marketing coordinator, or to a marketing director in charge of all marketing activities. Either way, the top marketing person reports directly to the CEO, if marketing is to have any impact within the organization.

The worst-case scenario, once again, has neither a marketing coordinator nor a marketing director; instead, all marketing activities are under the complete supervision of the respective department heads.

Businesses in the United States were originally headed by manufacturing executives. After companies began to produce more than they could sell, the new CEOs came up through marketing. When sales were high but profits began to decline, the MBAs took over to protect the "bottom line."

During the following days of corporate mergers, leveraged buy outs, and takeovers, the new leaders were schooled in finance. Undoubtedly, the next wave of corporate CEOs will come up through international trade and finance.

The time may come when a significant percentage of nonprofits are headed by marketing executives, but that is certainly not true today. Although marketing is becoming recognized as more than a necessary evil, membership directors, advertising and exhibits sales directors, fund raisers, and other marketing staff in nonprofits would be unrealistic to set their goals beyond that of marketing coordinator or vice president of marketing or development.

When there is a breakthrough, expect it to come first within institutions that elevate to CEO their development directors or chief fund raisers.

15. Coordinator or Marketing Czar?

Income-producing activities in nonprofits evolve as organizations grow. As more departments discover means of selling products or services to their members, or of fund raising, the greater need for marketing coordination or direction.

While nonprofit CEOs are responsible for determining their organizational structures, the sheer size and number of marketing activities may influence their choice of a marketing coordinator vs. a single executive who manages all marketing efforts.

In a newly formed association, member dues account for most of its income. An executive director, administrative assistant, and secretary juggle their time as they cover the government agencies and legislature, publish a monthly newsletter, and send out occasional mailings for new members.

The association expands by hiring knowledgeable people capable of preparing additional publications and special reports that benefit members and are appealing to nonmembers.

At this stage there is a need for a membership director. Although some associations opt for a computer-literate list manager, those intent on growth select their first marketing-oriented staff member to build the organization. A membership marketing person discovers new opportunities. Through planned, aggressive direct mail promotion new members are added, and current members retained. Publications and special reports are cross-promoted as inducements for membership and for sales to both members and nonmembers. If the association has an annual meeting, the membership marketing person can take over or coordinate registration sales, and may participate in exhibits sales.

A marketing coordinator is born.

In community-related nonprofit institutions such as museums, universities, or zoos, membership marketing may be in the hands of public-spirited volunteers. Although their services are invaluable, the addition of a membership marketing professional to coordinate planned membership efforts is a sure way of increasing patrons, alumni, or members.

This is also true of institutions such as hospitals that rely on fund raising rather than memberships. Volunteers can build the hospital to a certain point, but the combination of volunteers with marketing professionals merges the best talents of both for sustained growth.

As associations and institutions expand, there may be more marketing activities than a membership director can supervise. Magazines that sell advertising and cross-promote the nonprofit's services require someone to work with advertising salespeople and editors. There are special events to be promoted; sponsorships to be solicited; exhibits to be manned; and insurance, gift shops, and promotional catalogs to be cross-promoted.

Role of Marketing Coordinator

With open and complete backing of the CEO, a marketing coordinator can persuade department heads to work together on income-producing activities. The marketer is in no position to dictate to staff people who report to department heads nor to department heads who report to the CEO, but it can be done successfully.

Consider these examples:

- COORDINATING WITH MEMBERSHIP DIRECTORS
  —Assist in developing new potential member lists.
  —Help obtain books and special reports, special rate convention registrations, and promotional items from other departments as inducements to join the organization.
  —Assist in the preparation of new member advertising and estab-

lish advertising exchange agreements with similar organizations.

—Enlist the CEO to strengthen member-retention programs such as a quarterly report from the president to all or key members.

—If there are associate members, coordinate lists and contacts with advertising and exhibits sales staff.

- COORDINATING WITH PUBLICATIONS DIRECTORS

—Obtain books and reports for use by the membership department.

—Work with editors in placing and positioning advertising for membership, meetings and conventions, insurance, and promotional items.

—Assist editors in promoting magazines, newsletters, and other publications with exhibits at similar organization conventions and with advertising exchange agreements.

—Provide advertising salespeople with industrywide marketing information and coordinate their activities with associate members.

—Act with top management negotiators for insurance plans, telephone, bank card, and travel discounts to bring them in as advertisers.

- COORDINATING WITH SPECIAL EVENTS AND CONVENTION MANAGERS

—Assist with advertising and publicity by placing ads and articles in house publications and in other publications.

—Bring marketing information from publications' reader and purchasing studies for use in registration and exhibits sales.

—Assist in obtaining sponsorships for luncheons, dinners, coffee breaks, and entertainment events.

—Coordinate the organization's booth at special events or conventions with or without exhibits, for sales of publications, products, services, and memberships.

- COORDINATING NEGOTIATED SERVICES AND DISCOUNTS

—Act as liaison between commercial and nonprofit interests, so that all will benefit financially while also benefiting the members.

—Coordinate the promotion of insurance, credit cards, and travel discount plans through membership and convention registration mailings and through advertising.

- COORDINATING WITH GIFT SHOP AND PROMOTIONAL CATALOG MANAGERS
  —Assist with preparation and placement of advertising and promotion.
  —Cross-promote other organization products and services in shops and catalogs.

A marketing coordinator is, in effect, a bee that cross-pollinates the flowers within a nonprofit organization. By encouraging a joint effort among the marketing activities of various departments, the coordinator produces a synergism that increases the value of each to the whole. With no power and little prestige, it is a thankless job. A good marketing coordinator should be well paid, based on results.

How can this coordinating role be effective in organizations where each income-producing department is a separate profit center? That is even more difficult.

Procter & Gamble and General Motors are frequently cited as companies where each product must stand on its own. Procter & Gamble produces several detergent brands that compete with each other as well as with brands of other companies. Buick competes with Chevrolet, Cadillac, and Oldsmobile just as it does with Ford, Chrysler, and imported models.

When this principle is applied to nonprofit organizations, however, it may not work as well. Profit is not their primary purpose, as it is with commercial companies. Nonprofits can seldom afford the competitive atmosphere.

In organizations with separate profit centers, the obstacles to synergistic growth are difficult to hurdle. Marketing activities are nearly impossible to coordinate; the spirit of competition among departments is too great.

A strong day-to-day administrator at the top can make any type of organization effective, but what happens when the nonprofit has an "outside" executive where department heads report directly to the CEO?

Role of Marketing Director

Organizations with high-profile, freewheeling senior executives as department heads may grow to the point where they need the services of a marketing director. Many of these executives have reputations within their industries or professions. They frequently have their own constituencies, and tend to trample or ignore marketing coordinators. In that case, the only solution may be to hire a formidable marketing executive from the outside, one who also has a national or industry-wide reputation and is on an equal footing with the other senior executives.

All marketing or fund-raising activities could be placed under the direction of the marketing or development department, headed by the outside professional. This could exact restructuring of other departments. Membership services members and maintains lists, but does not engage in membership sales. Publications publishes newsletters, magazines, directories, and reports but no longer sells or advertises them. Convention managers plan the sessions and invite speakers, but registration and exhibit sales are under marketing. Telemarketing would be used extensively for all marketing and research activities, also as part of the marketing operation.

Under a marketing "czar," there would be no competing profit centers. All income from products, services, or events would funnel through the marketing department. That is power, however, unnecessary power. Fortunately, the marketing czar structure is cited as an extreme solution that might create even more problems.

Even the largest institutions and associations have evolved while maintaining shared marketing responsibility arrangements. Special events may be under a vice president/marketing, while fund raising that calls for personal contact with major donors is headed by a vice president/development.

Fund raising usually has its own department in nonprofits. This is particularly true of capital project fund raising where there is a specific building or planned expansion, along with a targeted goal date. Marketing activities other than fund raising can be managed by a marketing executive without upsetting the organizational structure.

Provided the marketing director is an equal among equals, respected by other department heads, it is possible for the marketing department to oversee income-producing activities even though they remain in their various departments. For example, with input from other departments the marketing department could produce all direct mail promotion and advertising for memberships, registrations, and exhibit sales. This would ensure a central creative theme reflecting the organization as a whole rather than its departments, and would stagger the mailings throughout the year through coordinated planning. Marketing could also be in charge of advertising trade agreements, exchanging space in house publications with other nonprofit publications, and exhibit space for advertising in trade publications. The telephone sales efforts would continue to be conducted by the membership and convention departments, and income would still be credited to them.

Although a marketing "czar" is an extreme example, there are nonprofits too large or unwieldy for a marketing coordinator with no authority. Those organizations have a marketing director who can coordinate income-producing activities with the strongest of department heads.

When income-producing activities are engaged in by more than one department, nonprofits can no longer afford to be without some type of marketing coordinator or director who has the open backing of top management.

16. Marketing in a Nonprofit Environment

Associations and other nonprofit organizations have accepted income-producing activities as vital to their existence. They are reaching out for new marketing opportunities that benefit their members and financially strengthen their organizations.

"Marketing" in the broadest term is just being discovered. Neither glamorous nor frivolous, marketing is a serious profession that requires intensive research, planning, budgeting, promotion, advertising, sales, and analysis. If taken seriously by top management, marketing will find its proper niche in a nonprofit environment. Taken too seriously, however, it can be disruptive, defeating the original purpose.

As an example, the East End Children's Workshop of Portland Maine is a private, nonprofit agency that provides affordable child care and family support services in the downtown Portland area. Children are from cross-cultural ethnic and income families who are charged on a sliding fee scale. The Children's Workshop is funded by state and federal agencies, and the local United Way.

Because of the recession and government debt, funds are being squeezed by all three levels—local, state, and federal. Consequently, the East End board of directors has turned to marketing to meet expenses. Their most marketable asset is a large, well-equipped kitchen. They are currently contacting other nonprofit daycare centers to provide luncheons at a reasonable price, with positive results.

If this were carried to an extreme, however, and more attention were paid to selling food than to meeting the needs of children under

East End's care, the increased income would be irrelevant because it would defeat the center's original purpose.

There are income-producing opportunities for nonprofit organizations, large and small. In its rightful place, marketing will benefit all concerned.

ACKNOWLEDGMENTS

It was pure enjoyment meeting with the people who assisted me in the development of this book. Most are real professionals who are contributing to the enhancement and growth of their nonprofit organizations. I would like to thank and acknowledge the following:

THE ADLER PLANETARIUM, Chicago, IL—Jessica L. Mackinnon, Membership Coordinator, and Lothair Studios (design).

AMERICAN ASSOCIATION OF RETIRED PERSONS (AARP), Washington, D.C.—Melinda J. Halpert, Dir., Membership Development and W. B. Doner & Co., Advertising, Baltimore, MD.

AMERICAN SOCIETY OF ASSOCIATION EXECUTIVES (ASAE), Washington, DC—Heidi S. Bowers, Book Editor.

LOS ANGELES COUNTY MUSEUM OF ART, Los Angeles, CA—Melody Kanschat, Head, Membership, Office of Development. Dalton Associates and the Museum Membership and Development staff should be credited for the "Georgia O'Keeffe New Member Mailing" and "Your Inside Track To Privileges, Priorities and a Private Party;" and "A Special Invitation For You" and "The President's Circle" letter and brochure were prepared and designed by the Membership and Development staff.

MARINE CORPS ASSOCIATION (MCA), Quantico, VA—Col. L. J. Piantadosi, Assistant Director, Maj. Terry L. Barnes, Marketing & Operations, Donna J. Boots, Bookservice Manager, and John J. Breheny, Circulation Manager.

NATIONAL ASSOCIATION OF BROADCASTERS (NAB), Washington, DC—Donna Leonard, V.P., Radio Membership.

NATIONAL ASSOCIATION OF CHAIN DRUG STORES, INC. (NACDS), Alexandria, VA—John R. Covert, Director, Communications and the Povich Design Group of Bethesda, MD.

PACIFIC WHALE FOUNDATION (PWF), Maui, HI—Susan Jo Eads, Membership Director.

PEPPERDINE UNIVERSITY, Malibu, CA—Robert Blair, Manager of Direct Marketing.

SAINT LOUIS ZOO, St. Louis, MO—Cynthia S. Sumner, Director of Development. Credit should also be given to those who developed the Zoo's outstanding promotional materials: "We're Here All Year" art director David Bartels, President, Bartels & Carstens, artist Braldt Bralds, theme IQ & Associates, and copy, Cynthia Sumner; "Do You Zoo? We Do" theme and copy, Dana Hines, President, Membership Consultants and artwork by Lori Majur; ZUDUS magazine editor Jerry H. Sears, design Chiow Communications and Charles H. Hoessle, Director, Saint Louis Zoo; *Visitors Guide* writer and editor, Emily Oseas Routman, Universal Printing, designer Kiku Obata & Company; *Zoo Friends MasterCard* copy and design by The Atkinson Group, artist Braldt Bralds, and credit card designer John Walsh.

SAINT JOHN'S HOSPITAL AND HEALTH CENTER, Santa Monica, CA—Dr. Vahe Simonium, Executive Vice President—Development, Roxanne Yamaguchi, Director, Marketing & Public Relations, and Susan Wilson, Director, The Jimmy Stewart Relay Marathon.

THE UNITED STATES-CHINA BUSINESS COUNCIL, Washington, DC—Roger W. Sullivan, former President, and Madelyn C. Ross, Director Publications and Executive Director, China Business Forum, educational arm of the Council.

I would also like to express my appreciation to Melanie Winans who assisted in preparing the manuscript and Charles Lean, Taft Group Editorial Director who provided encouragement and valuable assistance.